PRAISE FOR

DEAR ORCHID

"Powerful, haunting, and precise. Each of the essays and stories in Van Den Hende's collection—whether a three-page reverie of childhood's joys and tragedies or a candid peek into the life of a wounded hero—land with a piercing clarity."

— FIONA DAVIS, *New York Times* bestselling author of *The Stolen Queen*

"Prepare to be inspired, moved, and to find echoes of your own life within these pages. A truly remarkable read!"

— REBECCA ROSENBERG, *Champagne Widows* series

"*Dear Orchid* reminds us that tragedy can also open hearts and souls to lives fully lived in unexpected circumstances."

— SUSAN CUSHMAN, author of *Pilgrim Interrupted*, *John and Mary Margaret* and *Cherry Bomb*

"A delightful medley of memories and stories connected to the creative surprises and inspirations for her celebrated *Orchid* series. For fans of Van Den Hende's novels, *Dear Orchid* cannot be missed."

— SARAHLYN BRUCK, author of *Light of the Fire*

"With unflinching honesty, unexpected humor, and a voice both tender and fierce, Carol Van Den Hende reveals the complicated, beautiful ways we adapt, endure, and sometimes even thrive. *Dear Orchid* will linger in your mind long after the last page, like a bruise you keep pressing—not to hurt, but to remember you're still here."

— CHRISTINA CONSOLINO, award-winning author of *The Marriage Debt*

"A soulful collection of essays and reflections blending truth and imagination, *Dear Orchid* is a heartfelt exploration of how youthful wonder naturally matures into genuine wisdom. Through a captivating tapestry of essays, Carol takes readers on an inspiring journey of awakening, growth, and self-discovery, capturing life's rawest emotions with authenticity. Whether you've been on these paths or simply recognize the feelings they evoke, this book speaks to the universal human experience."

—HOPE GIBBS, author *Where the Grass Grows Blue*

"It's an honor to know Carol Van Den Hende. We have shared incredible life experiences. She has a rare gift for turning that richness into authentic stories."

— SGT. BRYAN ANDERSON, author of *No Turning Back: One Man's Inspiring True Story of Courage, Determination, and Hope*

PRAISE FOR THE

GOODBYE ORCHID SERIES

"Carol Van Den Hende never disappoints. Her books are full of rich characters, real challenges and deep emotion."

— KRISTAN HIGGINS, *New York Times, USA TODAY, Publisher's Weekly* bestselling author

"An engrossing, inspiring depiction of traumatized individuals growing amidst challenges."

—Kirkus Reviews

"An inherently compelling, impressively original, and deftly crafted novel showcasing author Carol Van Den Hende's distinctive narrative driven storytelling style...Especially and unreservedly recommended."

— Midwest Book Review

"An expertly crafted novel that will tug not just on your heart strings, but on your soul."

— KARIN TANABE, author of *A Woman of Intelligence*

"*Always Orchid* explores the power of love and perseverance in the face of trauma and discrimination. A heart-warming story with compassionate connections. Readers won't be disappointed."

— RACHEL BARENBAUM, author of *Atomic Anna*

Dear Orchid: Letters and New Beginnings—True Stories and Fiction filled with Heart, Humor, and Hope

by Carol Van Den Hende

ISBN Paperback 978-1-958223-07-9
ISBN Hardcover 978-1-958223-08-6
ISBN Ebook 978-1-958223-06-2

Published by Azine Press

TRUE STORIES & NEW FICTION

Dear Orchid

BY CAROL VAN DEN HENDE

Azine Press™

DEDICATION

To my aunt who shines with grace and strength in all her roles—as wife, parent, grandmother, entrepreneur, and humanitarian.

ALSO BY CAROL VAN DEN HENDE

Orchid Blooming

Goodbye Orchid

Always Orchid

Orchids murmur mysteries —

delicate and resilient,

orchids defy their stereotype

touted as a fragile species

fickle and frail

yet like each of us, dig deep to find
a web of roots,
the strength to gather nutrients from air,
a hardiness that endures.

Dear Reader,

Since time immemorial, letters expressed care for someone dear to us.

When I met Sgt. Bryan Anderson, I'd read his memoir about the explosion that claimed both his legs and his left hand. But sitting beside him, hearing his laugh, seeing his eyes crinkle with lightness despite everything—something shifted. I wrote him a letter, one I never expected to share. That letter became the first chapter of *Dear Orchid*, called "Still, You're Tall."

Writing to Bryan opened something in me. Maybe you've experienced this too, if you've ever wondered why certain stories stay with us. The impact of meeting Bryan made me ask: *Where does my tenderness for wounded heroes come from?* The answer pulled me inward, into the stories I'd carried since childhood. Into the memory of my father's illness. An unlikely friendship with a man who didn't speak. A dear secret auntie. These true stories form the letters in the first section *"Where I Begin."*

With the past awakened, I saw threads connecting moments across decades—across cultures, generations, and within each of us. In the section titled *"A Coterie of Orchids,"* you'll find personal letters drawn from my adult life: a train ride with the man I would marry ("Dear Mr. Blue Sweater"), a visit to East Berlin just weeks after the Wall fell ("Dear Berliner"), and inside the world of a post-punk nightclub from the 1980's. These too are true stories, offered as love letters to special people and moments in time.

In *"Meeting My Heroes,"* you'll get to know some of the real-life warriors who shaped my fiction. Their resilience—and generosity in supporting the *Goodbye Orchid* series—remind us that it isn't a mistake to meet our heroes.

Finally, the section *"Fate Chance Love"* invites you into the world of fiction. These six short stories are imagined, but still, they mirror resilience, compassion, and the redemptive power of second chances. While you don't need to have read the *Goodbye Orchid* novels to enter this world, you may find familiar echoes—characters and themes that continue to grow beyond the final chapter.

This collection is our place to spend time together: part time capsule, part homage, part behind-the-scenes glimpse into my creative process. Dear reader, this book is for you.

Welcome back. Or simply: welcome.

–CAROL VAN DEN HENDE

Whenever I am alone with you, you make me feel whole again …
Whenever I am alone with you, you make me feel free again.

– Robert Smith, The Cure, *Lovesong*

Contents

Still, You're Tall

"What matters in life isn't what happens to us but how we choose to react to it."

—Sgt. Bryan Anderson, author *No Turning Back*

2015, NORTH RIDGE, CALIFORNIA

Dear Sgt. Bryan,

You zip towards me, fast and fluid, like gravity had cut you a deal. I cross the street, notebook clutched tight, hoping the person who's survived so much still resembles the man I've come to know on paper.

Your porch blooms with pink petunias. Your wheels hit the sun-warmed concrete like punctuation, exclamation marks of movement. I see the gray tee stretched over your chest, the sunglasses perched on your close-cropped hair: anticipation tangled with reverence.

I cross the street, heart thudding from the weight of this moment. You lean forward in your chair like you can't get to me fast enough. It feels like we've known each other longer than we have—your story etched into the chapters of my manuscript, and now, in front of me, the real you.

We meet at the curb, that gentle concrete slope meant to ease transitions.

"How are you doing?" you ask, eyes steady on mine. No filler. Like you really want to know. Not small talk. A real question.

"I'm good. You?"

"I'm good too," you reply. But we both know we are more than that. We've survived things, overcome things, shared things.

You glance me over, from my black skirt to my skater high-tops. "You're tall," you say, certain.

"It's my shoes," I shrug, lifting a platform wedge to show you.

"Still," you say, unmoved. "You're tall."

It's not flirtation. It is fact. It is noticing. It is presence.

And I notice you, too—your tribal tattoo spiraling down one arm, your calm strength, the slight strain as your wheels bump the threshold of your front door. I see it: how carpet drags, how you can't quite clean your sunglasses, how everything asks more of you. And how you answer each inconvenience with a shrug and forward motion.

Later, I'd feel the ache of that—what you live with, what you don't show. But in that moment, we just are two people, meeting at the edge of something. We leave the Los Angeles sky behind and enter your home, not for the first time, not really. We've already met in story. This is just our physical forms catching up.

Inside, your dog and cat stir. "Hi Mya. Hi Ari," I say, petting them. "I brought them something." I proffer the gift-wrapped treat-dispensing toy. You glance at it, then nod for me to follow you through the house. I leave the package on a side table, a little disappointed—until later, when I realize what you didn't say: that twisting the toy open would be nearly impossible with one hand.

You wheel forward, pointing out rooms—the artist roommate's bedroom with chalk mandalas, the guest bath, then into the master. "I got this one," you say, "since the lease is in my name." I catch the subtext. You didn't get the bigger room because of your disability; you earned it.

In the ensuite bathroom, you gesture to the doorframe you had removed to fit your chair. "I told the landlord I'll reinstall it when I leave," you say, like it's no big deal. The bathroom looks ordinary. I ask about the tub—no roll-in shower?

"I just hop in," you say, demonstrating with a quick lift from your wheelchair. I see it now—the gymnast's body, the easy strength. You once told me you and your twin brother were high school athletes. It shows.

"Mind if I wash my hands?" I ask. "I'm allergic to cats."

You gesture toward the automated soap dispenser. Citrus scent rises as I scrub away dander. Later I'll see the same dispenser in your kitchen, another quiet adaptation you downplay. Some changes you speak about freely; others, you tuck into silence. I'll come to understand that you consider ramps and hand controls essential. Motion sensors and button hooks? Maybe they feel like giving in.

Back in your bedroom, we tackle laundry. I perch on your neatly made bed. "You take care of the hard ones," you say, tossing me a polo shirt. You wrestle a pair of shorts into a military square. As we fold, I recall experimenting with my morning routine one-handed while I wrote *Goodbye Orchid*; the awkward balance of my toothbrush on the vanity as I smeared Colgate onto its bristles, taking twice as long to wash my hair, and the frustration of fastening my clothes.

"I used to have a button-hook tool," you tell me. "Lost it in a move. Now I just use my teeth."

You grin wide, proud of your resourcefulness. Then, a mischievous spark: "Know what's missing from the wash?"

I squint at the pile. "Socks?"

You laugh. "No feet, no socks."

It hits me, even though I've read your memoir, seen you on TV. I've tried not to stare, not to focus on the spot where your prosthetic arm meets your elbow or the shape of your shorts. But here you are, disarming discomfort with humor. Refusing to let anyone—even me—fall into pity.

I think of the moment the improvised explosive device changed your life in Baghdad. Of the melted metal of your Humvee. Your

confusion. The dust. The friend with whom you locked eyes. The punchline you gasped through a collapsed lung: "Do you think I'll ever get laid again?"

Even at the edge of death, you reached for laughter. Sitting with you now, it's not your injuries that overwhelm me—it's your presence. Your composure. The clarity you carry like oxygen.

I ask the question I've been holding. "If you could change anything, what would you change?"

You pause. The air stills. Mya and Ari snuffle quietly from the other room. I wonder if I shouldn't have asked. Perhaps the question hits too close to the core, it's too personal.

You offer insight like a mantra: "I wish people wouldn't judge my life based on how I look. They say, 'I could never live like that.' Like it's better to be dead. I have a good life. I love my life."

Your gaze holds mine. And I know, bone-deep, that I'll carry your words into every sentence I write. You once told me, "Come see me. Spend a few days. I'll show you how easy I make it look."

And now you have. You've shown me everything. Not perfection. Not pity. But purpose. I look to your one whole arm. Your tattoo reads: LIVE. LOVE. THRIVE.

It fits. It's you. It's more than words—it's a way of being.

And never mind the pet toy. Never mind the carpeted hallway.

This—your presence, your humor, your unflinching truth—this is the gift.

WHERE I BEGIN, true stories from childhood

My Wild, Wild Twin

"I first caught the perfume of my wild twin by walking with muddy boots through wet grasses to my scrubby woodland den as a six-year-old ... The wild twin is not unique to me; you have one, everyone has one ... It is incorrigible, melodramatic, and has only your best interests at heart."

–Martin Shaw, author of Courting the Wild Twin

Carol and her best friend as children, playing the board game Sorry

The day we met, all I wanted was a tuna sandwich.

Your mom—barefoot, careful—approached us like someone trying not to startle wild animals. She laid down the platter as if coaxing us into trust. Wonder Bread, tuna, a touch of celery, maybe. The smell of mayonnaise always takes me back to that moment.

We crouched over a Sorry board game on the concrete porch, red and yellow pieces waiting to colonize, teaching children how to conquer each other politely.

I watched you, your flyaway hippie hair, oversized front teeth, with the unrestrained giggle of a six-year-old. You devoured that sandwich like you'd never been fed. Crumbs flew, mayonnaise smeared your lips, and I remember thinking: here is my wild twin. Not sunshine and roses, you were orchids and moonlight.

Our families rented town homes in a Maryland housing complex known as Whiskey Bottom. You grew up on Bourbon Street. I lived on Moonshine Hollow. What a place is called matters. Before we moved in, a salesperson explained the origin of the name, which dated back to the 1860s. "A distillery used this road to roll barrels of whiskey to the railroad station." His colorful backstory seemed designed to distract us from the military drabness of the squat two-story buildings in putrid yellow-green. For some families, these could represent a steppingstone to better days. Others seemed to skim the edge of civility, where a missed paycheck could spell disaster.

As kids, adults' desperation barely filtered through our consciousness. We felt ownership of our nearby sidewalks and streets, spending every blue-sky day exploring farther reaches of our neighborhood. I learned that you hated losing and cried easily, so I orchestrated our time together into an endless stream of amusements. I invented games with all winners and no losers, transporting us to make-believe worlds with storytelling. There is no greater imagination than that of two unfettered latchkey kids.

I was the freest the eleventh summer of my childhood. In a T-shirt, shorts, with a key around my neck, I ran carefree with my wild twin, scribbled adventure stories into my journals, biked through muddy woods, and slurped nectar straight from untamed honeysuckle blossoms. My parents were busy with doctors' appointments.

Together with you, my best friend, we gobbled up those golden days until the velvet sky had grown inky, for long hours past our bedtimes. We ran free on Moonshine Hollow and Bourbon Street—our addresses as prophetic as fairy tale names.

This was before we knew anything about heartache or how a certain fondness rests a switch's width from hate. What did we know? And, since we didn't know what we didn't know, we filled ourselves with our world, all sunshine, the scent of cut grass, and alarmed with crickets.

Every summer day felt as if it could last forever.

Until, after a long illness, my father died. I was lost in grief, then whisked away without goodbye. No time to explain, no closure, no last story spun from clouds. We never fell out. I mean who can fall out with the first runner-up for best suburban porn-star name?

I landed somewhere polished and privileged. You stayed in the cracked pavement of Whiskey Bottom. I kept rising. You began to fall. As children are wont to do, we lost touch.

Even so, I never forgot you, your family, or Whiskey Bottom. When we reunited, what mischief we could stir. You and your mom marked an early essential part of me.

Years later, searching for your name after my twins were born, I found it buried in a court document.

I read it twice, disbelieving.

Your children's father hunted you, obsessed with your blood.

When you spotted him in your house, you screamed, "He's going to kill me!"

In his hand glinted the sharp steel of a sturdy knife.

You stumbled backwards, cradling your infant. Your two toddlers clung to your legs.

They said you grabbed the phone.

No dial tone. The line was dead.

I read, hoping that the legal documents described another unfortunate soul.

Yet the personal details matched yours. Your killer had stalked you. You'd tried to run. You'd shielded your children.

Oh, my friend, could no one come to your aid?

Seventeen wounds.

I shed tears, for the time lost between us, for the years you wouldn't have, for your children.

Much later, I cried again—when I learned of your grown son's death. Twenty years old. A promising future. Gone by his own hand.

You're both lost to us now.

What I remember is your toothy smile. I treasure our photos. I recall our games and summer freedom, the sole keeper for both of our childhood adventures. Your mother exclaims with joy when I call. I imagine her eating tuna sandwiches. Only on white bread.

I tell her she made the best ones.

She tells me she loves me.

I say it back.

Life is capricious: wild twins, one path split in two. One blessed. One destroyed.

Goldie Forever

I. SUNSHINE AND HUNGER

Today's sunshine could melt a crayon. No juice. No cereal. No Daddy in the house. Just dry air and hot sidewalks. I draw sunbursts on the concrete, but the chalk crumbles like stale crackers.

And then—

You.

Orange like fire, fluffy as a dream. You pause at the edge of my patio, studying me like I'm a puzzle worth solving. A golden question mark with whiskers.

"Hello, kitty," I whisper.

You blink. You walk away. But you've already answered something I didn't know I asked. There can be miracles, unexpected surprises, and a connection between living beings that transcends language.

II. THE COMING

You come back the next day. And the next. Every time closer. I wait on the porch with scraps: Vienna sausage, half a slice of ham, Swiss cheese rolled in bread crust.

You eat without blinking. You are my first guest, my quiet teacher. Your purr vibrates the bones in my chest.

I name you Goldie. With my child's logic, the name's obviousness makes it perfect. Like naming the moon Round.

You learn to trust my chin scratches. We lie together on the porch lounge chair, the air thick with heat and invisible promises. You belong to me. Or I belong to you. It's the same thing.

III. THE DISAPPEARANCE

One afternoon, when I return home from school, you're not waiting on the chaise lounge for me. I circle the neighborhood with chicken cat treats in hand, calling your name. No orange flash, no marmalade mouser. By nighttime, I must go inside for bed.

The next day, you're still gone. And the next.

For weeks, I seek any sight of your furry ears, your jaunty step.

Until I'm forlorn with lost hope. Evening temperatures are beginning to drop.

I'm learning to crochet, so I stitch rows of blue ombre yarn into a sweater for you. My offering to bring you back.

And then, one afternoon—as I'm tossing jacks on the ground, not caring how they land—a faint cry pricks my ears. I pause my motion, straining to hear. An animalistic rumble. I stand, wanting to wish you into existence but afraid to be disappointed. Your utterances grow distinct, and with them, my hope. A repeated howl with urgency. A voice I know.

I abandon my game to run up the hill. Over the horizon, your tangerine blur streaks down the sidewalk headed straight for me. You're galloping full tilt, your melody of meows growing louder. You don't slow until you're in my arms. We hold each other with relief and joy.

I find my gift for you and slip the sweater over your head. You trust me enough to let me jimmy the blue tube over your torso. Its ridiculously small size squashes your fur flat and shrinks your size in half. I giggle and help you wiggle free.

You must be hungry. I fill your bowl with fresh kibble that scent the air with a meaty tang. You devour them like you haven't feasted for weeks.

IV. A BOXED HOPE

After eating, you follow me inside. I mentally prepare an explanation for Mama that the weather is growing chilly. She doesn't notice us or pretends not to. I tear open a shipping box, line it with towels to make you a cardboard bed. You accept the tight makeshift space of our bathroom without complaint. You curl inside the box like you've been waiting all your life for this moment.

Your fur smells like the wind. Your eyes are green-gold marbles. I whisper all my secrets into the folds of your body.

You are the softest place in the world.

V. THE SICKNESS

One morning, Daddy returns. His breath rattles. His face is a color I don't have a name for. Mama whispers about hospital visits, about allergens, about the cat.

I press my body against the bathroom door.

"No," I say. "He didn't mean it."

Nobody hears me.

VI. THE GOING

The ride is too short. You are in a box again, this one closed. I feel the warmth of your body on my legs, your weight shifting with every turn.

We pull into the parking lot of our old apartment. It's beige and blank, like a bad dream.

Mama opens the car door.

"I can't do this," she says. "You take him."

I lift the box. You peek through the top. Our eyes meet.

"I'm so sorry," I say. "Stay close. Stay hidden. Stay safe."

I grab a piece of paper and bring your box into the safety of the building foyer. I don't want to leave you. You crawl into my lap. I murmur all the things you've meant to me in all the ways I can think of. "Goldie, Goldie," I say again and again, so you won't forget your name, so you will always have a memory of my voice.

Even in this moment, when your future is uncertain, you exude calm and love, confidence that all will be well. You look at me. I'm sniveling and wiping my face with my sleeve. I tape the paper to your back, feeling your bony spine under my fingertips. To your credit, you never wriggle, you never complain.

You let me crayon the words "HELP ME" onto your torso, the saddest little missive, an inadequate poem to what a good cat you are. More than that. You are the kind soul who picked me, who loved me, who gave me so much when I had nothing. You gave me yourself.

A century passes.

When I finally walk away, I don't look back.

VII. THE AFTER

Weeks elapse. I leave food on our porch. I wonder if you can find your way back, miles over the highway. You'd granted me a miracle once before. I whisper your name into the grass and strain to hear your corresponding meow. It doesn't come.

I dream of apricot fur.

Sometimes, when the light is just right, I see you flicker across the yard—tail high, ears sharp.

I close my eyes and lie still, hoping you'll come curl into the hollow of my chest.

Hoping you'll know I never wanted you to go.

Epitaph: No evidence has ever convinced me to believe in reincarnation. Still, on one occasion, two ginger cats joined our household. One turned out goofy, the other skittish; neither possessed your regal demeanor or wise-soul eyes. I had my doubts. Even so, when they were tiny, I cupped them in my palm, smoothed their golden fur flat against their delicate ribs, and wished aloud into their furry ears, "Have you come back to me, Goldie?"

Dear Mr. Ten-Speed

You held a secret behind your tongue. I held one in my pocket.

They unveiled themselves in front of the Coca-Cola machine.

With your baseball cap pulled low, you hopped off your shiny ten-speed, the epitome of bicycle technology. Beside it, my banana seat bike looked like a doll's toy. You nodded at me yesterday, zipping by on your gleaming metal machine, past my handlebar streamers flapping in the breeze.

Today, you were on a mission. In three fluid strides, you loped over to quench your thirst. You hadn't deciphered that I'd just pulled off the heist of my eleven-year life.

I had just enough time to hide my implement of thievery, a broken branch, behind my back. But not the guilt and exhilaration that I could feel warring on my face. I would later recognize my emotion as remorse and resolve to never again take anything that wasn't mine.

For now, cans of Dr. Pepper sweated at my feet. I swept a generous hand to indicate the machine was all yours.

Accepting my offer with a polite nod, you stepped up to push the square plastic button for a Sprite.

Had you never used a vending machine before? With no money, of course nothing happened. Frustrated, your muscled arm gave the metal beast a shove. You couldn't win that battle but your strong physique looked like it could damage the steel.

My fear of being caught melted away. It didn't matter that you were older. You needed me to take charge (a good life lesson that I would take into adulthood).

I fished two looted coins from my pocket and slipped them into the slot. You see, earlier that week, I had purchased my favorite beverage and noticed that the sound of quarters dropped with a satisfying clink. Curious about the machine's inner workings, I peered through an opening in the front of the soda machine. My gaze traveled down the inky darkness and could just make out a plastic tub at the bottom. Silver overflowed the square collection cup, winking at me with a request to come out to play.

That pile of pocket change spelled freedom. I dreamt of Creamsicles from the ice cream truck and Baby Ruths from the vending machine.

Now, I had returned to the community center with my best friend, masking tape affixed to the long stick. One coin at a time, we had emptied half the machine's earnings by the time you arrived. We could afford to be magnanimous.

Your green and white aluminum can rolled down the chute with a satisfying thump. For the first time, you looked past my skinny legs and scabbed knees. Admiration crossed your face as you realized your underestimation. With one easy motion, you popped open the aluminum tab and lifted the can, toasting us like we were at a dinner party.

After a long gulp of liquid, you tipped your cap and ran a finger along your brim, pointing to the blocky letters that spelled out R-I-C-H-A-R-D in rainbow colors.

Understanding clicked.

Our whole interaction had been silent. For whatever reason, you didn't speak. Thinking back, I realized that whenever we'd see you around our neighborhood, you were alone. I wondered if you could use a friend.

After that, whenever we would see you outside, we would wave you over to join our sports games. Little by little, you grew comfortable tossing a ball around with us.

Once during a break from playing kickball, you introduced yourself to my friend's mom, sharing your name through the emblazoned hat that you donned everywhere.

One August day, we snuck in an especially vigorous game before dusk. We ended the match laughing, panting for breath, hands on our knees. As my friend ran to fetch the ball rolling down the slope, you looked me in the eyes and held your arms open. The universal invitation for a hug.

I paused, remembering school assemblies where police officers spoke about "Stranger Danger." Safety posters showed grown men with thick necks and dark eyebrows not unlike yours.

In a split-second that felt longer, I assessed your intent and the risk you could pose to a girl alone on a hilltop. You were close enough that I could smell your sweat from our games.

Yet you were no stranger. Sprite afficionado, graceful ten-speeder, kickball expert who would sometimes let two girls win. There was no malice. I let you loop an arm over my shoulders, nothing untoward. Like an ode, our connection sang to me in scores. Our closeness spoke a language of its own. It whispered that you had been lonely, perhaps separated from others because of your hearing or speech disability. Silently, you thanked me for giving you something special: friendship, camaraderie, understanding. I accepted you unconditionally. You appreciated feeling valued. You felt seen. You let go seconds or minutes later. It was an early lesson on the power of inclusivity.

Four decades later, I looked for you. My breadcrumbs of information were slight. With just your first name, and the town you had lived in as a twenty-something-year-old, I searched schools for the deaf and scoured yearbooks from the time period that you probably attended high school. One photo of an athletic young man named Richard

echoed your strong hairline and dark eyebrows. I found a phone number for this Richard plastered onto a Yellow Pages website and left a voicemail.

No response.

Wherever you are, I hope you're soaring on your racing bike. If you happen upon my writing, my third novel, *Always Orchid*, is dedicated to "Richard, who sparked my empathy for disability inclusion by listening with all his being and communicating with all his heart."

No secrets behind your tongue or in my pockets. Just respect.

Dear Luna Moth

At first, you startled me. You spread your enormous green wingspan on the corner of our front door, an unblinking orange eye emblazoned onto each appendage. Alone, I was the only one who noticed you. Your body expanded with each breath. Were you young, new to this earth, marveling at the hollow of the birch where you were born and fluffy clouds overhead?

I hope not. My conscience would fare better to think that you had enjoyed a full life.

You didn't fly away when I tickled the curled edge of your beautiful wing with a stick. Your legs shuffled a lackluster millimeter to the left. Were you resting on our door jamb, maybe seeking help?

I sat on the edge of our lounge chair and plucked at the wild garlic growing in our yard. Observing your stillness, I worried that perhaps you were ill.

An idea popped into my head. One person who seemed to know everything about entomology was Mr. Puglisi, our school science teacher. I recalled his jovial demeanor with relief. He would know how to care for you.

You weren't hard to catch. My mother helped me to shepherd you into a large jar, much bigger than the glass containers we used to house lightning bugs on summer nights.

I wondered what you might need and selected long tender stalks of grass to accompany you. Their dark green contrasted with your pale hue, which was as delicate as jade. It seemed like you blinked your insect eyes as a thank you to me.

That night, I kept you by my bedside, airholes drilled in the lid, a capful of water at the bottom of your jar, until I could carefully carry you on the school bus.

The next day, inside our science classroom, Mr. Puglisi greeted you with fanfare. "It's rare to see luna moths fully formed, since their adult lives are so short," he announced to the class, holding up your clear home for all to see. "This one is a beauty. They're considered giant silk moths," he explained.

In the bright light, you fluttered to life, as if roused by the attention. "Can you help him?" I asked my trusted teacher.

"I'll take care of him," he told me with a wink, and brought my jar to a back room.

My burden of keeping you alive lightened, I took my seat to listen to science class. Mr. Puglisi spoke about our insect collections, which would comprise half our semester's grade. We had until the end of the week to bring samples. I looked out the window, picturing you flying by like an unexpected green kite.

As Mr. Puglisi began his lecture, sharing the order of the planets, my mind attended to three things at once. I half-listened to the information about Venus being our sister planet, adjacent but uninhabitable. My stomach, meanwhile, wondered what the cafeteria would serve, as breakfast was never enough to keep me satiated until lunchtime.

The most pressing part of my attention was on Mr. Puglisi himself. He was pale, with dark hair, and skin so thin that it glowed translucent against visibly blue veins. On the first day of class, after he explained that we could shorten his long moniker to Mr. Pug, he told us something personal.

"I am a hemophiliac," he said. "It's a genetic condition where my blood doesn't clot. So, if I get a cut, it won't stop bleeding. You'll have to be careful around me. No jostling, no accidents."

My imagination pictured our art classes' gleaming scissors, storeroom staplers, and home economics' sewing machines. What if I handed Mr. Pug my homework and the knife's edge of the paper accidentally sliced the delicate skin between his thumb and forefinger? Would he gasp, clutch his hand, and fall onto the school carpet, a pool of dark liquid spreading around him until all five liters had emptied?

I knew something about the vulnerability of men succumbing to illness, as I'd overheard whispers of a serious disease ailing my father. Against this backdrop, Mr. Pug's disorder seemed tragic. His life could be cut short at any moment.

Yet he was the cheery guy who signed our yearbooks across two pages, starting with MR PUG, then finishing with LISI on the backside, each bubble letter oversized to match his personality.

My inner thoughts were interrupted by the lunch bell. We filed into the cafeteria, which smelled like gym socks and bleach. Ladies in hairnets served us pale rectangles of pizza, melted mozzarella atop a soggy crust. What might you be eating at this time, dear Luna Moth? Did Mr. Pug keep special sugary sap in his lab? I didn't know at the time that adult luna moths emerge with only vestigial mouth parts and no digestive organs, never eating but living on the fat they had stored as a larva.

After my final French class (*au revoir, professeur*!), Mr. Pug ambled towards me, carrying an object. As he drew closer, I recognized the yellow supply box that he had asked each of us to bring at the beginning of the school year.

His expression glowed with pride. "Here's your moth," he said.

I looked around. *Where?*

He bent down and began to lift the box's yellow lid, a number 2 pencil inked on top. Wait, I wanted to say, thinking you would fly

loose from the unhinged box, your haphazard path wandering the school hallways.

But no creature flitted from the box. No wings pulsed with each breath. No bright eyes to thank me for green stalks of grass.

Inside, on a rectangle of white foam, your jade green wings and orange eyes lay spread eagle and still. A sharp pin pierced your soft body, holding you aloft.

Mr. Pug's words reached my numbed ears. "He didn't succumb easily. It took me thirty minutes with chloroform to suffocate him."

I gasped. *Suffocate him?* I wanted you saved, not stuffed. For the half hour that I was devouring cardboard pizza, you were suffering.

Mr. Pug closed the lid over your lifeless body and handed your coffin to me. He walked away looking disappointed that I didn't seem overjoyed. I stood motionless even though I needed to hurry before school buses would leave on their afternoon routes.

One more drop of childhood innocence dissipated. I wanted to help beautiful you. But Mr. Pug saw you as something to preserve, even if the cost of doing so was to cut short your life.

By the time I had met you, you had already spent three to four weeks as a larva, molting several times. You'd already grown as a pupa for another two to three weeks.

Luna moths only live seven to ten days as adults. Scientists say your sole purpose during that week is to reproduce, that a male can detect a single female pheromone as far as six miles away and will travel that distance to produce offspring.

Literature calls you rare, beautiful, and ephemeral.

Mythical lore says that you represent transformation.

My fervent wish is that you could transform back to a wild creature, free to soar.

I shut my eyes, hoping that you spent your sole week with your wings buoyed by warm wind, and that your antennae, among the most sensitive in the world, luxuriated in the scent of fresh rain and wild garlic.

Dear Literary Grandpa

What language was closest to your heart?

Your native tongue from Kunshan? Mandarin? Or, after forty years in America, had English found its way in?

You weren't one for big declarations, but I knew you cared—because you spoke to me in stories.

You never talked much about your past. But I caught glimpses in your habits: how you saved twist ties and bread bags, how you grew quiet over certain memories. It was years before I learned you'd been separated from your infant daughter when China's borders closed. That loss, I think, lived in your silences.

Instead of telling your story, you showed me how to love words.

One of the most magical spots in your New Jersey home was the bookshelf in your finished basement—second only to the eat-in kitchen scented with tea eggs and sticky rice dumplings.

One summer, you brought me downstairs and granted me Christmas in July.

"My company let us take the extra books," you said, pride lifting your voice. "You can have as many as you want."

I imagined your job in publishing like Willy Wonka's Chocolate Factory: alphabets swirling through pipes, stories pouring off conveyor belts. I studied the colorful spines on your shelves—some titles in relaxed cursive, others in sharp, upright fonts.

I picked up *The Black Cauldron* and hesitated. "It's for nine- to twelve-year-olds," I said, worried it was too hard.

"That's okay," you said. "You're a good reader. You can have any of these."

With your blessing ringing in my ears, I carried my first armful upstairs. I passed the garage, where your son's German Shepherd whined. I loved that dog, but at that moment, books called louder. I sprawled on the fuchsia plastic-covered sofa, the one reserved for adults, and read the afternoon away.

You sat nearby, paging through your Chinese newspaper and a well-thumbed Bible edged in red, a satin ribbon marking your place. You didn't interrupt me. You understood the hush that reading requires. Maybe you felt it, too.

Years later, after my father died, you came to our Whiskey Bottom town house. You studied me with a blink as slow as tai chi. Then, like a magician, you pulled a fat paperback from your suitcase: the *Scribner-Bantam English Dictionary*. You had inscribed it to me.

You knew I was grieving. But you also knew what would soothe me: words.

I read that dictionary the way others read novels—from page one. Each entry felt like a miniature story. In its calm order, I felt your presence.

That dictionary still sits in my office. The spine is cracked at the word "mom."

In your nineties, you surprised me again. When I visited you and Grandma in your California assisted living home, you pushed a cardboard box across the Formica table.

"I've been writing," you said, eyes sparkling.

Inside were cassette tapes, each labeled in your neat, slanted script.

"It's the story of my childhood," you said. "I recorded it since you can't read Chinese."

I was stunned. After all these years, you'd found your voice. You spoke into that tape recorder about your life as a curious boy, before the political upheaval, before the silence.

That was your final literary gift. Not just a story, but *your* story. Recorded in Chinese, the language of your first home. The language of your earliest wonder.

When I hear your voice on those tapes—scratchy, sure—I hear the same care that once filled your basement shelves. I hear the quiet love behind every book you gave me. The gentleness in the gift of a dictionary. The tenderness in your final recordings.

You didn't speak love. You *wrote* it, *read* it, *recorded* it.

And all along, you gave it to me in a language we both could understand.

Dear Secret Auntie

We only met once. But I won't forget you.

You were just a baby when one decision altered the course of your life. Your plump cheek was nestled against your wet nurse's chest when your parents (my grandparents) agreed to send you back to your hometown in China. The plan was for her to care for her sick husband and continue nursing you. It was supposed to be a short trip. You would return to Taiwan as soon as things settled.

That temporary boat ride became a near permanent exile.

The year was 1949—a moment of profound upheaval. The Kuomintang, backed by landlords, elites, and middle-class families, was losing ground to Mao Zedong's Chinese Communist Party. Did your parents sense how close the tides were to turning? Did they hesitate at the dock, wondering if they were making a mistake?

On October 1, 1949, Mao stood atop the Gate of Heavenly Peace and declared the founding of the People's Republic of China. By then, you were already in Jiangsu Province. Within weeks, all travel between mainland China and Taiwan ceased. No letters. No boats. No return.

One decision. Your life forever changed.

Your wet nurse, newly widowed, couldn't keep you. She placed you with your paternal grandmother. If your grandma was anything like your father, I imagine her as gentle and kind. But she didn't get to raise you to adulthood. When she died, your uncle—labeled a former landowner—wasn't even allowed to give her a proper funeral. The old world was gone, and everything it stood for was being dismantled.

Your family's privilege became your burden.

You bore the punishment meant for others. At school, were you mocked? At home, were you hungry? Your uncle was reassigned as a janitor, your aunt left to boil gravy for dinner when there was nothing else to eat. Still, that wasn't enough. Because your parents were overseas, considered traitors, you were eventually sent to the countryside for hard labor—ripped away from the only family you'd known. I hope that your life held moments of joy—a beautiful sunset, a gesture of kindness.

The fragments of your story that survive—gathered like grains of rice scraped from an empty bowl—tell of unspeakable hardship.

You came of age during the Great Leap Forward, from 1958 to 1962, when misguided agricultural policies caused mass famine. You were eleven to fifteen, the age when children dream. But instead of dreaming, you were surviving. While crops rotted in fields, an estimated 15 to 55 million people starved. Were your arms thin, your belly swollen? Did your body forget what satiety felt like?

You were born in 1947, the Year of the Pig. In Chinese astrology, Pigs are honest, generous, warm-hearted. You were also a Fire Pig—meant to be passionate, ambitious, full of energy. In a just world, you would have lived a life of joy, surrounded by abundance.

Instead, your childhood was shaped by hunger, grief, and political shame.

But you endured.

Years later, your parents—now living in America—found a way to bring you and your husband over. It must have felt like a miracle. A reunion long-delayed. A door finally opened.

And yet, the trauma lingered.

I'm told that even after arriving, even surrounded by siblings and nieces and nephews, you didn't feel like one of us. You withdrew. You felt, perhaps, that too much time had passed. That too much had been taken.

My eldest aunt shared that you didn't even feel worthy of being introduced as her sister.

Eventually, you didn't return our family's calls.

Dear Auntie, I ache for what was lost. For the childhood you never had. For the stories you couldn't tell. For the silence that grew louder with time.

They say time is a great healer. I hope it brings you peace. That somewhere, perhaps now, you have found a place where there is always enough. Where you are seen. Where bowls of rice are unending.

In my heart, I hold onto the image of you as the truest version of the Chinese Zodiac Pig—kind, compassionate, full of quiet fire. A survivor. A symbol not of shame, but of strength.

A Handful of Rice

A STORY OF SECRET AUNTIE

"Like silt deposited on the cogs of a finely tuned machine after the seawater of a tsunami recedes, our experiences, and those of our forebears, are never gone, even if they have been forgotten."

—Dan Hurley, *Discover* Magazine on behavioral epigenetics shaping us across generations

1959, KUNSHAN, CHINA

I was born in the Year of the Pig. All I wanted was a handful of rice. It was dusk, the safest time to move through the town unnoticed. Most families were inside for the evening meal—if they were lucky enough to have one.

I slipped out through the side door of our once-grand house, now divided to shelter sixteen families. I kept close to the murky canal I'd lived beside all eleven years of my life.

As I passed the darkened windows of what had once been our family estate, I thought of Grandma's stories—how, before I was born, our family had owned the entire block and lands beyond the

river. She spoke of servants who carried platters of pearl meatballs and peeled lychee fruit. I had never tasted either.

I turned into a narrow alley few people used. This was Yang Ayi's street. She used to be our family's wet nurse, mine and my sister's before me, before my parents left for Taiwan. She had once told me that Baba was always reading, and Ma loved to laugh.

I counted the doorways: one with a crying baby, another strung with drying laundry, a third where my uncle had once bought eggs still warm from the hens. Yang Ayi's door was fourth. A sign outside read "5"—chosen to avoid the unlucky homophone for "death."

She had warned me not to visit. She didn't want the Red Guards accusing her of fraternizing with former landowners. Even stripped of our property, our history alone could endanger her. But I had no one else to turn to.

I found her squatting inside, washing a few green beans in a shallow bowl. A scarf covered her head.

Not wanting to startle her, I greeted her formally from the doorway.

"Aiyah," she sighed, looking up. But her eyes softened. She beckoned me in and closed the door behind us, shutting out the world.

She handed me a raw green bean, still dripping. I ate it, stem and all. The house smelled faintly of her: slightly sweaty, warm, familiar.

"You've grown tall," she said, eyes resting on my bony arms, my too-short pants, my thin-soled cloth shoes. "Are you eleven now?"

"Yes. Just last month."

She used to visit on my birthday, back when things were better. She had no children of her own. Illness had taken her daughter and husband. Their deaths had delayed our return to Taiwan—and by the time we were ready, the borders had closed. The last boat left Shanghai in October 1949. We were stranded.

"You're a Pig," she said. "That's lucky. You'll have a good life."

She always said that. She also said, "Your parents wanted you to be with them."

But today didn't feel lucky.

"My grandmother is sick," I blurted, and tears followed. Sweet Nainai, who had taught me to hold my head high when other children teased me for being abandoned.

Yang Ayi's mouth tightened. She pulled out the only two chairs in the room and sat beside me.

I reached into my pocket and held out Nainai's special brooch—a gold bird of paradise, its wings made of jade, its eyes tiny garnets. "She wanted you to have this."

She held it up, turning it toward the light. "Oh my. This is generous."

She knew how little we had left. Most valuables had been seized and redistributed. Before I left, Nainai had pressed the brooch into one of my hands. "For Yang Ayi," she whispered.

"Your uncle is still at home?" she asked gently. Every second I stayed, I put her at risk. Young people were joining the Red Guards. They listened. They reported.

I nodded. My throat was too tight to speak. My uncle had hugged me last night, his eyes red, before disappearing into the dark to find medicine. Or food. My empty stomach rumbled with the thought of sweet rice balls.

Our last meal had been a thin soup made from wild celery. My aunt placed it between my cousin and me. "I'm not hungry," she lied, giving us each a spoon.

My uncle now worked as a janitor. My aunt made up games to distract us from our hunger. I wanted to help them. I found my voice.

"Ayi, do you have any rice I can take home?"

I knew she'd understand. My aunt and uncle lived under scrutiny. They had family overseas. They were tested for loyalty at every turn. And of course, there was never enough to eat. Former landlords faced the harshest punishment. Reform through hunger.

"I carry my Little Red Book," I added, as if that would protect us. "I recite the Chairman's sayings at school."

"Dear child," she murmured. She got up and shuffled to her small kitchen.

She opened the pantry. The shelves were nearly bare—just like ours. Still, she reached into the back, searching.

So much rode on what she might find.

This was before Grandma's death, just days away. Before officials would tear me from my uncle and send me to the countryside for hard labor. Before I would learn what starvation really was. Before I would lose the only family I'd ever known.

She returned with a small satchel of rice in one hand. In the other, an envelope.

"Your parents wrote to me," she said, handing me the rice paper bordered in red and blue.

I held my breath. The calligraphy-worthy characters on the envelope were unmistakable—my father's handwriting.

"Thank you," I whispered, clutching the rice. And for the first time in a long while, I let myself hope the Year of the Pig might still hold some luck for me.

A COTERIE OF ORCHIDS, true stories from young adulthood+

The orchid is the wild poet of the plant world—its verses whisper across jungles, mountaintops, and forest floors. With over 28,000 known species, no other family of flowers sings with such vastness, such daring diversity. Each orchid is a living metaphor, a fleeting miracle sculpted in color and form. Some wear robes of celestial beauty—striped like tigers, speckled like stardust. Others lean into the strange, bearing tufts of hair, swollen textures, and ruffled grace, like creatures born from dreams or myths.

What binds this unruly chorus of blossoms, this infinite gallery of shape and splendor? In a world where rules dissolve, one truth endures: the orchid's most intimate secret lies in its heart. There, the flower's masculine and feminine energies entwine—not apart, but fused into a single, sacred structure known as the column. It rises like a prayer from the center of the bloom, the breathless union of opposites, a kiss of form and function so complete it feels like love incarnate.

In the language of flowers, the orchid does not merely speak—it seduces, it confesses, it dreams.

In a world full of roses,

be an orchid—

unique and extraordinary.

Dear Roller Twin

Which one of you picked us? Did you have a plan, or do you possess that elusive twin understanding, intuiting your desires without words?

The roller rink was packed with teenagers, typical for a Saturday night. Under the violet and red strobe lights, I couldn't help spotting the pair of you. First you, with a slighter build, an inch taller than your doppelganger. You glided through the crowds, smooth as a cool breath, free as air, slipping between novices without disturbing their wobbly ankles.

Your companion sped around the rink on rented skates, eating up the laminated floor with aggressive strides, his grey tee darkened under his armpits.

I was a regular, my elliptical path nearly as graceful backwards as forwards.

In that darkened theater of teen wants, legs pulsing to the beat of Prince's Purple Rain, I had variously met college students from nearby William Paterson University and 23-year-old skating fanatics.

Your flirtation started from afar. A slight nod of your chin. Then when you noticed me noticing you, you amped up your skating moves, your long legs crossing over each other, as fluid as walking on ice.

Do you remember seeing my friend and me skating to the side for a break? We took turns dipping our shared steak-cut fries into yellow nacho sauce, standing on the carpeted rest area which emitted a whiff of damp feet. You came over first, your velocity instantly slowed by the industrial carpet.

Under the fluorescent lights, I got my first clear look at the pleasing symmetry of your features and the fullness of your brown hair.

"Hey," you said.

"Hey," I responded.

"Want a fry?" my friend asked, thrusting the red and white paper boat towards you, its white lining spattered with oil stains.

You freed one of the fried potatoes, yellow cheese clinging to one side, and gobbled it down like you were hungry.

Your compadre chopped a path over and stopped before us, panting. "This is my brother," you said.

"You're welcome to our fries," I said, a teen form of a greeting.

We chatted over the greasy potatoes, their salty goodness stinging my nose. You shared that you were twins from a neighboring town of Wayne.

"Identical?" I asked.

"That's the number one question we get asked," you laughed. "And the answer is yes."

Our snack nearly consumed, you asked if we had plans after the rink closed.

After?!

"No," my friend said.

"Let's hang out," your brother suggested.

So, you both caught a ride with us in my friend's mom's car. We told her you were friends from high school, and she dropped us all off at my house. Except we couldn't go inside with boys we'd just met at ten o'clock at night.

"Show us your neighborhood," you proposed.

The four of us wandered down the street towards the town park where just a few summers ago, I had spent my days making macrame potholders. My friend and I lazed on the gazebo swing and told stories about a rock band that our schoolmates had formed.

"What's down there?" your brother asked, pointing towards pavement leading into the woods.

My friend hopped up, leaving me swinging alone. "A bike path. We'll show you."

The two of us followed my friend and your brother into the inky forest. We kept walking until streetlights, far behind us now, faded to pinpricks. The smell of wet leaves surrounded us.

Our light chitchat grew silent as we penetrated deeper and deeper, past trees that grasped at us with gnarled branches. The pavement faded to nothing until we were padding along a bare dirt path. I'd never traversed so far into the forest. Nothing was recognizable. No sign of a house, a road, any civilization was visible for the full 360 degrees around us. Moonlight reflected in puddles left from yesterday's rain. We skirted their edges, aiming to keep our shoes dry.

Your brother led the way until a splashing sound interrupted the silence. "Crap," he said. We neared until we could see him shaking one foot like a dog kicking leaves off its hind haunches. We halted, unable to see how far the bog extended around us. The composting foliage sucked at my heels.

My friend giggled and twirled her hair, a nervous response.

"How about we get you home? What time are your parents expecting you?" I asked, realizing how far we'd come, not just into the woods, but socially. Our isolation contrasted with the relative safety of the crowds at the roller rink.

You tipped your head back so that the moon cleared the shadows off half your features, your thick eyebrows, sloping nose, a hint of facial hair like you hadn't shaved in a few days. Your Adam's apple bobbed along your elongated neck. "The thing is..." you began.

Your brother cleared his throat, a warning. But you kept going. The truth is slippery and couldn't be stopped any more than you could catch water with your bare hands.

"Our parents aren't expecting us. We're in juvie," you said, each word seeming to be leaden with sadness.

This wasn't a phrase I'd ever learned in my honors English class. "Juvie?" I asked, puzzled at the foreign word.

"Juvenile detention center," you spelled it out for me. I could hear embarrassment color your voice. "We're not supposed to be out. We escaped."

Holy hell.

"Escaped?" my friend squeaked.

"Are you, like, *convicts*?" I asked. So many questions. For one, which direction had we come from?

The silver light of the moon revealed your anguish. Your words emerged low and earnest. "It's not like that. We messed up. We shouldn't have been locked up."

My friend and I slid a sideways glance at each other. *Locked up.* We were in deeper than we had ever been. This was a whole new level compared to harmless flirtation with one of the "burnouts" who offered us smokes outside the school back doors.

Before we could ask the next logical question, a loud crack erupted from behind us, like the snap of a branch being stepped on. None of us was moving, so it couldn't be us. The sound had emanated from the direction we had come through the woods.

Your brother lost his cool. Never mind his wet shoe. "Cops. They found us," he grunted, his panicked mind jumping to conclusions. "RUN!"

He took off. As if you were invisibly connected, his motion spurred you into action. First, you looked to see if I was okay. I gave a nod and followed fast. My friend huffed behind me. Neither of us were star students in our Physical Education classes. But the fear of law enforcement on our heels spurred us to speed ahead. Not that we had done anything wrong. Or had we? Were we now accomplices to escapees?

My feet flew under me, as light as when you first take off your rollerblades after a night of skating.

Your brother led the way, ahead of the pack. Until he slipped and cursed. "Stay back," he called, rolling onto his side.

You helped pull him up and guided him to sit on a fallen log. I could see how much you cared for him, the way you hefted his weight against your shoulder. You must've been spent, not just from skating and the run but the emotional burden of being a fugitive. At that very moment, there were likely adults hunting for you.

"Watch out. It's muddy here," you called over your shoulder, your chin indicating the slick ground.

My ears pricked at the normalcy in your tone, even though nothing was normal about this night. It hit me with a shock again. The two of you, articulate and neatly dressed in well-fitting tees and jeans, seemed like our peers, not troubled youth.

The woods exhaled the susurrant sigh of leaves rustling in the breeze. No one was chasing us. No sticks cracking. Either we had lost them when we bolted helter-skelter, or we'd been spooked by nothing more than ghosts.

My friend and I joined you two on the makeshift log-bench. Who knew how late it must be.

A cricket chirped, accompanying the rasp of our ragged breathing.

"Did you get hurt?" I asked your brother.

He shook his head. "No, I'm alright. It gets really muddy ahead."

You turned to my friend and me. "Are you okay?"

You were close enough that I could smell a little sweat mingled with the scent of soap. I leaned against your shoulder. "Yeah. But being with juvie runaways is exhausting."

Everyone chuckled, giving into the much-needed levity.

We sat in the deepening darkness. No footsteps. Just the song of a lone cricket and the smell of dirt all around us.

"If there's no one following us, let's start heading back soon," I said.

A few moments later, I stood, and the others did too. Your brother listed towards you, limping from his fall. As we walked, his stride evened out. Now that you'd admitted your situation, you sketched out the main plot points of your lives: your mom obliterated with alcohol, your dad gone, assigned to different foster homes, and running away to reunite with each other. Your story had the sad tinge of an after-

school TV special. You were kids without the self-agency to right the injustices heaped on you.

"That's really tough," I said. "At least you have each other."

The route back seemed faster than the one we took. We moved backwards from the depth of the woods onto the paved trail. With relief, I spotted the gazebo just visible in the dim moonlight. It looked beautiful.

You and your brother hoofed away on foot in the early morning hours, before the sun had pinked the skyline. Leaving behind indelible memories of clean-cut boys who had surprised us by being runaways and then surprised us again by being decent fellows.

Wherever you are, may you still have each other's backs.

May you think of us along moonlit paths.

RUTGERS UNIVERSITY NEW BRUNSWICK, NEW JERSEY

Dear Film Jim

I fell for you the way some people fall for waffles, which is to say completely and with wild abandon. How you pronounced "film," punching up the single-syllable word with a double-beat, like you'd emigrated from Scandinavia, or some other such place that favors long drawn-out vowels.

You'd caught up with me after a lecture and matched my stride. "How did you like fi-ilm class?" you asked. It might've been the bright rays blinding me after exiting the dark auditorium, but when I turned to see the source of the deep voice, the twitch on one side of your full lips gave you a bemused expression, like we already shared an inside joke.

We chatted, me walking towards the bus stop and you heading to another lecture hall. I learned that you were from a town twenty minutes from campus, not Scandinavia after all. We'd agreed it was unbelievable how much emotion Charlie Chaplin could convey in a silent movie. I had recalled the comedian eating his licorice shoes until he became ill. Before we parted, you asked innocuously "Which dorm are you in?"

"BAM," I said, the shorthand for the buildings called Busch, Allen, Metzger. Each dorm features four walk-up flights. Each floor houses dozens of rooms.

That afternoon, you found my place. "Jim!" I exclaimed in surprise as you sauntered down my hallway. To this day, I don't know how you conjured the magic of finding me. I introduced you to my roommate. We talked about school for some foggy long minutes, then you left,

leaving me kind of fluttery inside and also as mystified about the purpose of our conversation as during our initial meeting.

The back of your head, your thick dark waves, muscular shoulders clothed under a white tee, and tight rear under gym shorts had barely disappeared around the corner of our hallway before my roommate whipped around to stare at me.

"Oh. My. God," she said, enunciating every syllable like she had just taken a drama workshop.

"What? He probably needs someone to help him with homework."

"Do you really think someone that smart needs help with fi-ilm class?" she asked, her voice eviscerating me with sarcasm. She even captured your Scandinavian vowel quirk.

"You think he's smart?" I asked, knowing the answer.

"Forget smarts. He is the hottest guy I have ever seen. Like ever," she proclaimed, a statement of fact needing no confirmation from me.

Honestly, I *had* noticed. But naive me had inferred innocent motives to your interest.

At our next lecture, you came to sit beside me. "What *film* are we watching today?" you asked, your demeanor as cool as James Dean while your smile warmed my insides.

I told you that I could not remember if it was Fellini or some other classic director. The theater lights dimmed, hushing the class and preventing further conversation. Your forearm lay on our shared armrest, grazing my wrist when I lifted the attached table to take notes. The opening credits rolled on a movie called *Fanny & Alexander*. In Ingmar Bergman's swan song, he told the story of Swedish siblings whose standoffish stepfather punishes Alexander for his overactive imagination.

The austere house and magical shop where the brother and sister live were shot from a child's perspective, giving the setting an otherworldly feeling. The motion picture was so long that we couldn't even watch the full theater version in one class. After dismissal, you sauntered beside me and explained that you would have to run but that you would have a surprise for me later.

The anticipation of knowing that I'd see you again thrummed through me like the musical score to a denouement.

You didn't disappoint. You came to gather me from my fourth-floor walk-up in the Metzger building and we flew down the steps, leveraging the speed of gravity. I pictured you during your first scouting trip, visiting each building in alphabetical order, scouring each floor from first to fourth, asking for a student by my name. A hundred plus doors later, you found mine. Yet, when you had arrived, you seemed completely unflustered, not a bead of sweat in sight.

Outside, a sleek Honda motorcycle awaited us. "Have you ever ridden?" you asked. I shook my head, abashed at my lack of experience, and a little frightened by the powerful machine.

You guided me, gently settling a helmet over my head to protect my skull. You hopped on, steadying the motorbike with a wide stance, and then instructed me to swing a leg over the leather seat. Once I was in place, you looked over your shoulder. "Put your arms around my waist," you said, firm but kind. This was the closest we'd ever been. An intimate position in which the curls of your hair poking out from under your helmet tickled my neck, in which my fingers could trace your ribs. I caught your musty scent. Then the bike roared to life under us, vibrating. This wouldn't be our last adventure. As we hurled forwards, I instinctively abandoned my tentative grasp for a full-on hold, my arms clinging to your six-pack abs, the side of my face, in its fiberglass encasing, pressed into your back.

"You okay?" you shouted into the air, your words whipping by me. *Was I okay?*

"Yeah!" I yelled back and squeezed my eyes shut.

I only knew each split-second as it thundered through me, the rumble under my seat, the roar in my ears. The glory of being wholly present. All consciousness fell away: the blurred onlookers, our school campus, my whole past and my unknown future.

Dear Surfer Jim

Did you own a pair? Did you know where to shop for footwear? Did you ever get turned away from a business for arriving barefoot? Ironically, one of the things I don't like to see are feet. They vary in their weirdness, knobby or plump, blue-veined or distorted with bunions. I avert my eyes when online banners show gnarled yellowed nails advertising a fungus ointment. Your feet didn't bother me though; tan and well-built like the rest of you, nails neatly trimmed in contrast to your wild blond curls waving down to your muscled shoulders.

I never told you about my aversion. Rather, I asked, amusement in my voice, "Do you *ever* wear shoes?"

You stuck out your hand to shake mine, striking a surprisingly professional stance in contrast to your shirtless torso and beach shorts, "I'm Surfer Dude. And yeah, I wear flip flops on dates."

This line led to our first meal together at a long-standing establishment, Tumulty's Pub on George Street. During the period that we studied in New Brunswick, the downtown district exuded a seedy feel, filthy napkins blowing like tumbleweeds after empty chip bags and the occasional used condom.

I hadn't been looking for romance. Yet with you, I could sense the potential for adventure behind every wave of laughter and new idea. Without being consciously aware of it, adventure was likely what I was seeking at college. During my high school years, I grasped slivers of freedom, furtive slips of time with forbidden boyfriends, stolen school days window shopping in New York City's West Village, and nights grooving in dance clubs with my likewise underage friends.

But university flung the doors of possibility even wider. I debated existential questions with roommates, lying on our hard dorm beds, until the light of dawn crept through our dusty windows. Dormmates banded together to explore fraternity parties. Anything seemed possible. One day, a friend was recruited right off the street to walk as a model in designer Patricia Field's spring clothing show.

Even in the midst of a thousand moments, that dinner with you stands out in my memory as a singular experience. We entered the dark wood-paneled cave of Tumulty's restaurant. Deep brown timber scored the walls in a near-black crisscross pattern, seeming like the polar opposite of your good-natured disposition, in direct contrast to your sun-bleached hair, clean and angellike around your beatific smile.

A waitress escorted us to an elevated booth. We slipped into our facing seats, her glancing down from your ombre polo top (likely the only collared shirt you owned?) to check to see if your feet were shod. My eyes followed her gaze and confirmed that you had donned your "date-ready" sandals.

Unlike my engineering classmates who were endlessly running from the computer science lab to the medical school library for studying marathons, you took your time. You unhurriedly memorized my face, asking about me, showing no urgency to order food, simply fingering the edge of the hard plastic menu. The way I remember it, there was nothing lascivious about your expression. I felt seen. You wanted to know not just about my studies but about my hopes. Did I tell you about writing that night? Had I even comprehended what my decision would lead to when I agreed to major in engineering instead of English? Could I have guessed that writing could reemerge at a later time in life, like a cicada nymph maturing underground for seventeen years before unfurling fully formed?

You talked about catching ocean waves, the freedom of flying over foamy surf, your voice bright in that dim dungeon of an eatery. "We're going to do something magnificent. I can feel it," you vowed. Then you described your dream of sailing across the Atlantic.

I imagine you now, captain of your days, your curly locks whiter with age, the tough soles of your feet planted on a boat's wet deck. Your clear eyes are still as blue as the Sargasso Sea. Whatever port you anchor in, the people around you sense your purity and good conscience, as calm as the unbothered surface of the wide ocean on a windless day.

Like quiet vessels on diverging paths, we sailed apart at some point. There was no ill will, never harsh words. Only fond memories. Whatever seas you are cruising in life now, Surfer Jim, I wish you easy waters, warm rays, and shoeless days.

Dear Handsome Hansen

You carried the demeanor of an Irish prince stripped of title: regal in carriage, head ducked in humility like a young Hugh Grant in the movie *Notting Hill.*

When my freshman college roommate introduced us, you looked at me through your Harry Potteresque wire-rimmed glasses, your blue eyes as clear as if your every thought would shine transparently into the world.

"Hey," you said, peering at me from beneath your flop of brown hair.

"Brennan lives on our floor," my roommate said.

"Near the girls' bathroom, so I usually know about any late-night escapades," you said with an impish grin.

"Did you hear me on Saturday night?" I asked, remembering a boisterous fraternity party ending in the wee hours of the morning.

"Was that you?" you rejoindered with a laugh, deep and genuine and then explained you were on your way out. With a wave, you disappeared around the corner.

I would've never believed that someday, you would teach me about a disease from biblical times.

The next time you passed me in our shared hallway, you greeted me with a grin. "Busy day?" you guessed, pointing at my overstuffed school backpack.

"Wednesdays are killer. Chem, Chem Lab, and Calculus."

"Chemistry's not my subject but I'm decent at math. Let me know if you need help."

"Thanks. What's your major?"

We chatted about your study of Economics. You asked where I had gone to high school. In return, you sketched a vague description of your well-to-do hometown, swiping the air as if it only existed in an imaginary realm. You hinted at complicated relationships with your family, then deftly evaded personal questions as effectively as an aikido master sidesteps direct blows.

Your blue eyes didn't translate to transparency after all.

We began to bump into each other in our dorm hall. You would stop by my room to ask about my roommate and my classes or inquire what we were doing over the weekend. You were an upper classman. My freshman innocence was intrigued by your enigmatic ways.

One January evening, you came by later than normal. I was already dressed in my sleepwear.

"What are you wearing?" you asked, eyes wide. I looked down at the pink thermal long johns that my aunt had gifted me at Christmastime. The soft fabric stretched over my slender legs and skimmed my taut torso. Many girls wore their loose sleeping T-shirts over leggings outside of their rooms so it wasn't rare for those of us in the same hall to see each other ready for bed.

"My pajamas," I answered.

"Pajamas?!" you asked, your tone conveying disbelief. You strained to pull your gaze away from me. In a strangled voice, you bade me good night and left. I understood from your gaping stare that the form-fitting pjs my aunt hoped would keep me warm had made an impact on you. I went to bed feeling a sense of power. Later, I would learn who actually held power.

You returned to my room the next day, a moth drawn to pink thermals. I was sitting at my brown study carrel. Every student was assigned this type of sturdy desk, a single shelf up high and a fluorescent light shining below it. This time, I was sporting the outfit I had worn to that day's lectures: a boat neck top, jeans, and high-top sneakers.

It was common practice to leave your door ajar if you were amenable to visitors. You leaned into my open room and rapped on my door jamb. I glanced up from my Calculus textbook to take in your pale face, resplendent and unencumbered.

"What are you studying?" you asked.

I waved you in. "Math. Your favorite," I said.

You leaned down to peer over my shoulder at the page of integrals. You were close enough that I could feel your breath against my neck. Your hand brushed the side of my thin cotton shirt.

I flinched instinctively. "I'm ticklish," I warned you.

College kid that you were, your face curved into a devilish grin.

Did you know how much I hated being tickled? As much as anyone would despise something done against your will. Even the thought of wiggly fingers nearing my tender obliques could trigger a shudder.

My nervous system was dialed to a hyper-sensitive level.

You ran a finger down my waist. "Here?"

"No!" I shrieked, wanting you to stop.

My giggle, and perhaps a memory of my pink-wrapped curves, awakened something mischievous in your expression.

Talk about conundrums. When you're laughing, it appears from the outside that you're having a good time. And that's me when I'm tickled. My diaphragm pumps out air involuntarily. I'm guffawing, out of control, gasping for every breath. Those are the same reactions to an uncontrollable fear response. When I'm tickled, I'm sucking air so hard that I can't speak. I'm being violated, my body touched when I don't want it to be. But I can't say the words because I'm laughing too hard. Not a fun happy howl, rather an out-of-control roar. Like a sneeze you can't stop.

"How about here?" you asked, fingers provoking waves of irritation along my abdomen.

I jumped out of my seat. You followed, your grin indicating enjoyment.

All five fingers ruffled my shirt. Laughter burbled out of me, not in humor but the start of panic.

"I hate–," I started to say. But now you had stoked my tender abdomen with alarm on both sides. I backed up and tripped on my desk

chair. You followed my tumble to the floor, merciless. Peals of anguish were rippling from my gut, sounding like the opposite of what I felt. I scooted my legs away from you, backing into my closet. You crawled on your knees following me, your torturous hands relentless. I pushed you hard; my actions couldn't slow your grasping my tender sides.

I couldn't breathe. I couldn't speak. This was the days before students talked about "consent." Inside my head, I was shouting. All I could do was claw at your arms. As slight as your build was, you were overpowering me with your strength. My nails dug into your forearms, trying to tell you through my actions what my throat couldn't. My nails have always been strong. As a kid, I could grow all ten of them into long ovals, shining like pearls. They were useful for digging up dirt, pinching off dandelion heads and today, I could feel them embedding into your flesh, imploring you to halt.

Finally, something wild in my gaze, my cries growing animalistic, broke through your pursuit.

Both of us inside my closet, you finally backed up, panting almost as hard as me. I hurried upright, scurrying into my room a few feet before I could speak.

"Why didn't you stop? Didn't you feel me digging into you?" I asked, breathing hard, upset.

"Digging into me?" you repeated, standing as well.

"Yeah, into your arms." I pointed towards your hands, those torture devices. I didn't know at the time that tickling has been used as an actual torture method throughout history.

Concern passed over your face. You dropped your chin to view the red marks on the tender inside of your wrists, each shaped like the half-moon of my fingernails. Your pale skin was raw with wounds. I felt badly that I had hurt you. Yet my breathing hadn't fully calmed; my sides still agitated with fear.

The room grew quiet. There was something more. Something that you weren't ready to share.

You finally spoke. "I don't have feeling in my hands," you said, not meeting my gaze. You started through my open door. Over your shoulder, you gave me one more clue. "I have Hansen's disease," you said and then retreated, disappearing down the hallway.

This was before the days of ubiquitous internet. No Wikipedia. No Mayo Clinic website. I had never heard of Hansen's disease. But your creased brow indicated something serious.

An hour later, you returned, each red mark on your wrists glistening with salve. You handed me a paperback with a soft red cover, the serif lettering reminding me of fantasy novels like *The Black Cauldron* that I had read in my younger years. "Here," you said. "If you want to understand me more, read this." And you departed again, the mystery deepening.

The title stated *The Chronicles of Thomas Covenant the Unbeliever Book One: Lord Foul's Bane*, by Stephen R. Donaldson.

I changed into my pink thermal pajamas and began to read in bed. The story started with the main protagonist, Thomas Covenant, walking into town to pay his phone bill in person. His wife had divorced him, leaving with their child. Neighbors had moved, to stay away from him. The local supermarket delivered his groceries, to avoid him coming into the store. Nerve damage had reduced feeling in his extremities.

He was being ostracized because he had been diagnosed with Hansen's disease. Better known as leprosy.

Irish prince Brennan with the blue eyes and cloak of privilege was a *leper*? I had only read about the condition in the Bible. I didn't know it was a real malady still existing in our modern day.

I searched my mind. Leper colonies in ancient texts quarantined contagious patients to prevent spread of the bacterial disease. No other references in my knowledge bank.

In the book, Thomas Covenant is called on a hero's journey to save an alternate world. He's a reluctant hero, one who questions how he can hold any power when he's been outcast, considered unclean.

As I read deep into the night, I realized that you likewise vacillated between growing close to anyone and departing on your own terms, before someone else could leave you. You had resorted to vague responses to avoid being rejected.

By the next time we passed each other in our dorm hall, I had already investigated the basics of Hansen's disease in our university medical school library. I knew that modern day medicine could treat the bacterial infection, and it was unlikely to be transmitted. Leper colonies that still existed were voluntary places that provided a sense of community rather than mandatory places for sick people to be banished.

"I finished your book. I'm sorry. Are you okay?" I asked, hoping that my voice could convey my genuine care.

"Yeah," you mumbled, staring at the tips of your oxford loafers.

"I can return it. You want me to get it?"

"No rush. You can just leave it at my door. Whenever." Your gaze avoided mine like we were magnetic poles. You rotated towards your room, posture tense like a racer awaiting the starting gun.

"Are your wrists healed?"

"They're better." You flipped over one pale forearm, its pink marks faded. You shivered an involuntary shudder and closed your eyes. I knew too much.

"I better go," you mumbled, and bolted away.

You avoided me after that.

After all, I had glimpsed the most vulnerable part of you.

Although I tried to engage you multiple times, we ended the school year without another meaningful conversation.

Aikido master or not, you hadn't been able to dodge revealing this secret.

Brennan, if we meet again, keep your fingers wriggle-free. I've largely outgrown my fear of being tickled. Just as I hope you've learned that your Hansen's secret won't lead everyone to forsake you.

Dear Mr. Blue Sweater

Was it a hand-me-down? Had you found it in a thrift bin? You boarded my New Jersey Transit train wearing khaki pants, loafers, and a decidedly unfashionable oatmeal-blue sweater. Scratchy wool hairs sprouted from its worn surface, its V-neck revealing a button-down shirt underneath. But you also sported a warm smile and a pile of books, not a common accoutrement at eleven p.m. on a Saturday night.

So, when you indicated with a nod that you wanted to join my row of three orange seats, I scooted towards the window, leaving an empty space between us. In that moment regarding you, I instantly absorbed an array of impressions. You seemed genuine, trustworthy, warm, and—I don't know how else to put it—safe.

That night, your literary choice made all the difference.

"Is that John Irving's new book?" I asked, my tone trending towards excitement as I eyed the patterned grey cover printed with the words *A Prayer for Owen Meany.*

"Yeah, he spoke at my sister's college graduation, so I wanted to read it," you said, your voice new to my ears. Yet you seemed familiar to me, like we'd known each other a long time already.

As the train swayed, you spoke over the clatter of the tracks to tell me about the book and your work as an engineer. You made me chuckle, acting out scenes from the British comedy troupe Monty Python. "It's just a flesh wound," you cried, mimicking the tone of the Black Knight after King Arthur dealt a blow that was clearly more than a nick. I always said if there was one quality I needed in a person it was a sense of humor.

In most ways, you weren't like other men I was drawn to. In those young college days, I tended towards creatives, artists, an edgy style, and a hint of angst. Still, I was disappointed to hear that you'd be getting off at the next stop to change trains.

Then your big brown eyes lit with an idea. "At night, I work at Brentano's Bookstore to help pay down my student loans. Just give me your address and I'll ship you a copy of John Irving's book."

The train slowed to enter your station.

You were a stranger. Yet your demeanor seemed kind. I calculated a split-second judgment call. I took the pen you offered and scribbled an address into your notebook. Not my actual physical address, but a safe, central location for mail.

You studied my college P.O. Box address and granted me a smile. "Bye," you said.

I waved as you left.

It wasn't goodbye.

A week later, I visited my post office to find a brown paper-wrapped book. Using your return address, I sent a thank you card. Then you wrote me a letter telling me about yourself. You mentioned your parents' impending divorce. I replied, telling you about my life at school and expressing sympathy for the hard time you must be going through. A few letters later, you wrote to ask me for my phone number.

We spent hours talking, trading stories both heartfelt and funny. One day, you suggested that we meet for dinner.

On our first date, our clashing sartorial choices almost ended our evening prematurely. Your conservative 3-piece blue suit seemed to promise a professorial lecture rather than a fun-filled meal. You later admitted that my outfit gave you pause. My minidress nipped at the waist, black-and-white striped stockings, and shiny patent shoes with oversized bows seemed quirky.

Luckily, those first impressions soon melted away. Once we sat down for dinner, it felt as though there wasn't enough time for all we wanted to say and do. We prolonged the evening by imbibing drinks at my friend's bar, laughing and talking all the while. Then we rode the train to New Brunswick to dance at my favorite college hang-out, *The Melody*, until its two-a.m. closing time.

When did you sense this wouldn't be the last time we saw each other?

Our early correspondence now lives together with keepsakes from our travels, alongside handmade pottery from our international assignment to China, our twin's grade school finger paintings, and marble tiles from our two-year home renovation. On a treasured bookshelf, two copies of *A Prayer for Owen Meany* have spent the decades of our marriage tucked side-by-side, like a long-time wedded couple.

Somewhere among the stuff we've collected over the years, if we dig deep enough, perhaps we could even find your scratchy wool oatmeal-blue V-neck sweater. I no longer question your fashion choices. Your favorite "uniform" of a sky-blue button-down shirt, khaki pants, and loafers suits you. As does your kindness, care, and always, your good humor. Thank you, dear Mr. Blue Sweater, thank you for our laughter and our own stories. Enough to fill books, our hearts, and a lifetime of memories.

1989, EAST GERMANY

Dear Berliner

Do you remember how you felt when you could finally travel from East Berlin to the Western side? Do you tell the story of us handing you money, saying in our broken German, "We don't need this anymore"?

Back in 1989, my husband-to-be and I were barely adults, having met when I was in college. You were probably a handful of years younger, a schoolgirl. This was our first overseas trip together and we booked flights on the now defunct Pan Am Airlines. We had planned to visit family in the Netherlands and art institutions in Paris. But when news reached us that the Berlin Wall had fallen, we felt compelled to make our way there. We met young people from Europe, Asia, and North America who held the same idea. Buses, planes, and trains arrived in Berlin full of idealistic youth.

During our overnight Eurail Pass trip on the train known as *The Berliner*, the atmosphere shifted once we crossed the border into East Germany. Conductors woke us every several hours, demanding our papers. That is, until we neared Berlin, an island moored within East Germany. Then we were left to slumber in peace. No intercom announced our arrival into the West Berlin train station. We later learned that the East German guards hoped that passengers would miss their stop. Their motivation was that once we traveled deeper into the Soviet bloc, we would have to pay fines for violating our visas. Luckily, we woke as the train pulled into Berlin's central station.

First, we visited Checkpoint Charlie, the place where guards had prevented citizens from crossing since the wall's formation in 1961. Two weeks before, the East German director stated that he would

no longer be operating the station, and that Germans were allowed to travel freely through the border. Thousands flocked to celebrate this moving symbol of democracy's rise.

We arrived to find people dismantling the concrete structure. We still own a piece of the wall, as gray, misshapen and crumbling as the ideology of keeping people apart.

Once night fell, we decided to cross the border to visit East Berlin. We completed the visa paperwork and each exchanged the required $10USD worth of currency into East German marks. Then we walked through the gates into what had once been part of the same city. Yet, the buildings seemed grayer, the stone more worn, people's faces more heavily lined, as if gravity weighed more newtons in Communist Germany.

With money to spend in our pockets, we sought a place to eat. Unlike West Berlin which featured avenues of commercial shops, grocers, and restaurants, the darkened windows that we passed in East Berlin bore no intelligible signs.

Approaching us, an elderly woman pushed a collapsible shopping cart, her gray hair wrapped in a scarf. As she neared, she broke into an enormous grin and leapt a few inches off the ground, enough to click her heels together before landing solid on her heavy black shoes.

We laughed with her, feeling her joy.

"Hello," my husband said in his elementary German to the woman. "We were wondering if you might be able to help us. We are seeking a place to eat. Do you know somewhere we could spend $10?"

I understood enough of their hand gestures and my husband's nods to interpret that she felt $10 was a lot of money. She pointed deeper into the city center and left, humming to herself.

We began walking in the direction she indicated. My future husband spoke as we strolled arm in arm. "She said to have any chance of spending that money, we will have to eat at the most expensive place in the city: the Opera House. And there's no guarantee what food they will have available."

A thrill of anticipation shivered up my arms. "An opera house? Am I dressed fancy enough?"

Humorous hubby assessed my Benetton sweater, dark pants and raincoat. "I don't know but there's no way to change, so let's go."

We walked on, a feeling of adventure lightening our steps. The old woman's good mood buoyed us.

We passed darkened buildings. Fog settled over the night, seeming to fit the gloomy feel of the city.

Soon, we were skittering up the stone stairs. A German placard greeted us, entitled Deutsche Staatsoper. "This is the oldest opera house in Berlin," he translated for me.

Inside, we asked the tired-looking waitstaff for a table and were seated in the cavernous room, beside one of the elegantly swooping columns. The size of the space soared with grandeur but every surface appeared to be worn down to dull gray. The place smelled like a damp dog.

We were handed a "menu," a handwritten piece of paper protected by a grayed plastic sleeve which seemed to have earned its wrinkles, pockmarks, and cigarette burn holes over decades of reuse.

"What do you have that is vegetarian?" my husband asked.

"Mushroom soup," the waiter replied.

"That sounds good," I said, hungry from walking around all day.

"Do you have bread? Cheese? Salad? Vegetables?" hubby asked.

The waiter's eyebrows wiggled like they wanted to rise with incredulity, then decided they were too tired to do so. With a disinterested air, he finally responded. "We might have bread."

"Two soups, bread, and wine, please," hubby ordered.

The waiter left and we chatted about our day.

"I'm so excited to be in the nicest restaurant in the city," I said. I should've paid more attention to the warning signs and tamped down my expectations.

The soup was placed before us in low shallow bowls, the liquid as ashen as the restaurant's porcelain dishes.

Famished, I stirred the gray water with my oversized soup spoon and sipped my first mouthful. Two mushroom pieces swirled with the motion of my silverware.

One swallow could have sent the head of Campbell's Research & Development function screaming into a nearby bomb shelter. I silently vowed to never take for granted the comforting consistency of a red and white can of Cream of Mushroom soup. A stale crust of bread swirled into the murky fluid helped to add some substance to our watery meal. I filled my belly as best as I could.

Despite the bland dinner, we left with good cheer over our adventure. Outside, the fog had deepened, giving the streets the mood of a Sherlock Holmes mystery.

We chanced upon a college-aged woman we had met on the train that morning. "You have to see this tower," Mangai said, leading us to the next block where a huge turret, lit from below, rose into the sky. As she and I looked up at the structure, unsure where it ended in the thick fog, hubby snapped an ethereal photo, one that seemed to capture the other-worldly feel of that singular night. One that we've not experienced again.

She said goodbye and we turned back towards the checkpoint where we'd entered.

Mangai and Carol in East Berlin, November 1989

As we neared the exit, we met you. Even at the most expensive restaurant in the city, we had only been able to spend half of our exchanged German marks. We spotted you, a young girl sporting pigtail braids over each shoulder. Your spritely steps spoke of newfound joy.

We paused to speak with you. You stopped before us on the sidewalk and returned our smiles, face turned upwards as if seeking to be helpful. Perhaps you thought that we could use directions.

"Hello. We were wondering if you could help us. We have this extra money. We don't need it anymore. Do you have any use for it?" humorous hubby asked.

With each subsequent sentence, your eyes grew wider, your jaw unhinged farther.

"*Extra* money?" you asked, as if this adjective had never before been strung together with the concept of funds.

"Don't *need* it?" you queried, puzzled at this possibility.

"Do *I* have any use for it?" you asked, your questioning tone wondering aloud if we didn't understand what we were saying.

Hubby removed one German mark as a memento for our scrap book and pressed the remaining cash into your hand.

You automatically closed your palm over the bills and stared at them as if we had performed a magic trick.

"Good evening," we said and walked towards Checkpoint Charlie. We needed to cross the now-defunct border to catch our train to France.

You called out. We turned to see your face split into a state of glory that cleared the nighttime fog and lifted the gray city into a rainbow of joy. "Thank you!" you said, your voice ringing clear with gratitude, not just for the money, but for the greater gift of freedom.

Mother

Mother

One of my favorite characters in my *Goodbye Orchid* series is Phoenix's mother. The formidable Veronica takes a central role in her son's recovery. In developing Veronica, I imagined the ways my own mother was protective towards me.

My mother was, inconceivably, just twenty-one years old when she gave birth to me. Photos showed her as an attentive mom swaddling me in blankets, taking her responsibilities in stride. Ultimately, she struggled in adulthood and left this world too soon.

I marvel at the myriad mothering figures in our lives, from friends to relatives. In that reflection, I realize that I too have multiple mother figures to thank. That list includes aunts, teachers, grandmothers, my mother-in-law, and friends' mothers.

Some of my earliest memories belong to my childhood best friend and her mother Lena. She took me under her parental wing, treating her daughter and me as one. She would halve tuna sandwiches on squishy Wonder bread for our lunch and then drive us in her pickup truck to a nearby 7-Eleven store for icy Slurpee drinks.

One day, a neighborhood boy unloaded his cadre of curse words in a whispered hush. Buzzing with this insider knowledge, we imprinted

them in oversized chalk letters on the sidewalk. They made us feel grown up.

After the colorful forms filled the pavement, Lena emerged from her front door. She studied our childish scrawl, one hand on her hip. She could've scolded us. She could've yelled. We held our breaths, both excited and fearing the prospect of getting an outsized reaction.

A whisper of a smirk passed over her lips. Then, in her thirty-something year old wisdom, she spoke to us without judgment.

"Do you know what this means?" she asked, pointing at what turned out to be one of the milder expletives.

"No," we admitted.

"That?" she indicated a more heinous one.

We shook our heads, eyes wide at her even demeanor.

One by one, she explained the meaning of each word, with the dry tone of an underclassmen professor. By stripping away their mystery, her matter-of-fact lesson diminished their power.

My friend and I looked at each other. We'd evaded a lecture. In its place, we had internalized a feeling that we would never forget. *Respect.* Even at that tender age, Lena trusted us. And with that respect, we learned that we held responsibility for what we uttered. More than that, Lena loved us enough to tell, not yell. We loved her right back.

In my teen years, my mother's sister filled a void and showed me how an organized, disciplined household ran. Despite her petite stature, she is a formidable matriarch, an enterprising entrepreneur, a tough negotiator. *Resilient.* She showed me how to do it all.

I still felt like an ingenue when I met my future mother-in-law. A beautiful woman with dramatic dark eyelashes, she favored clothes in purple hues, like royalty. Photographs of her as a devoted mother seemed too good to be true. In yellowed albums, her children are outfitted in homemade Raggedy Ann and Andy Halloween costumes. Pictures show her hand-dyeing wool, spinning it into yarn, and crafting wall art on gigantic looms. She entertained, raised three children, and assimilated into The Netherlands, her third home country.

Her sweet nature was nearly unshakable. Right from our initial meeting, she welcomed me with warmth. When I confided that I was nervous to prepare my first Thanksgiving meal, we stood side-by-side, making the family's famous curry-chestnut stuffing together. She penned pages of Polish and Dutch recipes in her rounded, left-slanted handwriting. This bound collection is so treasured that one of our sons has already requested that we bequeath it to him.

Despite being thousands of miles away, she and her husband traveled to celebrate major occasions with us. There was our wedding, birthdays, the twins' christening in the U.S., and their first Holy Communion in Beijing. When our boys were toddlers, my husband and I won a Bahamas getaway. Grandma and Opa volunteered to babysit. After three days, we were eager to see our babes again. We rushed through the front door and cast our luggage aside. The twins were enjoying a meal from their highchairs. They bounced when they saw us, proud to demonstrate what they had learned from Grandma and Opa. Arms aloft, they crashed their covered sippy cups together. "Chee-yahs!" they shouted with glee. "To Gwandma's booze!"

Over our decades together, Grandma was quick to laugh and reticent to dole out criticism. She taught me about parenting through her actions. A gentle soul, she observed and listened without judgment. We felt her encouragement over weekly phone calls, and care through every handwritten note and parcel. *Kindness*. As our boys grew up, Grandma's bright-yellow chick candles and bunny tablecloths brightened our Easter celebrations. At Christmastime, we would think of her as we unpacked her velvet ornaments that she had hand-encrusted with beads and jewels.

When our twins turned five, two scrolls arrived through the mail. We unrolled beautifully inked images of cats frolicking in the sun, decorated with details specific to each boy. My husband hired a gallery to lovingly frame them. In our household, they're treasured more than any art that we could purchase.

Before my second novel was released, we traveled to The Netherlands, knowing that my mother-in-law was gravely ill. We settled into the kitchen for some tea, and I presented her with an early copy of *Orchid Blooming*. She admired the pretty book cover and pointed out the pink orchids that were blooming on the shelf above her sink.

I encouraged her to flip open the signed copy to the dedication page.

She did so but then she patted the empty pockets of her purple sweater, sounding disappointed. "Oh, I don't have my glasses."

"I can read it aloud," I offered. With her nod of assent, I shared the words that I had written in her honor. "To my mother-in-law, who lights up the world with her art, and shines compassion into our lives with love."

"Oh, oh," she exclaimed. With wet eyes, she pulled me into a hug.

Later that year, the illness that she'd faced with incredible fortitude took her from us too soon. At her memorial, I spoke alongside my husband, his siblings, and others. I strove to convey what her decades of kindness meant to me. When I shared the story of Grandma and Opa babysitting our toddlers, the audience in attendance didn't sound surprised that she enjoyed "Gwandma's booze." I concluded by asking everyone to raise an imaginary glass in her honor. With arms raised high, they joined me in wishing "Grandma, who loved purple" a hearty "chee-yahs!"

I'm filled with the image of women around the world, each holding up the next generation. Our shared humanity glows with the beauty of motherhood. I radiate a little of what each of my mother figures have shared with me, that I can embody a bit of kindness, respect, resilience, and more.

NEW YORK CITY

Dear Mutant's Cat

Tell me, when did you know that you'd get swept up in Mutant's mishap?

Don't get me wrong. I know that your pet parent was an upstanding human. His tongue-in-cheek name was self-proclaimed in good fun. He loved his job at an agency who (mostly) accepted his six-foot bulk, penchant for body hardware, and weekends spent in metalcore mosh pits.

Things started to go awry when his beautician friend asked to practice her newfound hair coloring skills on him.

"Sure," he said, peering at his brown roots starting to show under his white-blond locks.

One morning before his workday, he perched onto the toilet lid in his bathroom while she brushed a chemical onto his short spiky hairdo. Despite the strong smell, you sat prim, tail wrapped around your haunches, watching the proceedings. You liked being near Mutant, interested in his goings-on.

They chatted as she glanced at her watch, measuring the requisite time. "This new line is all natural. It's made with plants and can even be ingested," she explained.

She picked up the bottle of product to show him. As she read the back label, her eyelids fluttered. "Uh-oh," she said.

"Uh-oh?" Mutant asked, itching his scalp with his fingertips.

"Get in the shower, quick!" she shouted.

She grabbed his arm and made him bend his six-foot frame over the tub's edge. She guided his head under the spout and ran cold water over his tresses, rinsing again and again.

You figured he was in trouble when she leaned back and started to blubber. "I'm so sorry!" she cried, and ran out of his apartment, leaving all her supplies behind.

He straightened and faced his medicine cabinet mirror. There, you both saw the reason she had fled.

Instead of his 80's retro Billy Idol-like spiky white hairdo, his waterlogged mane shone green. He dried it with a hot blast from the hair dryer. The result wasn't a dark forest green but a neon shade that rivaled a blinding tennis ball. *Me-wow.*

You heard him mutter to himself. "What can I do? I have to get to work. We have a client presentation this afternoon."

Later, Mutant explained to a friend over the phone what had happened. After he clocked in at the office, he entered the conference room where they were practicing the client pitch. All conversations ceased. Every set of eyes turned to stare at him.

He watched them take in his faded Ministry T-shirt and ripped black jeans. Then all their gazes landed on the tennis-ball-hued sprouts atop his head. His best friend covered her mouth to keep from laughing aloud.

His boss, though, didn't see the humor in the situation. He pulled out his wallet. "Here's $200. Go to a salon and get your hair back to what *you* consider normal. Don't come back until it's done."

He tried to hide the heat he could feel rising in his face and did as he was asked.

When Mutant came home that night, he threw open the front door and stomped to the kitchen. He was normally a good-natured pet parent. Tonight, he slammed the cabinet door where he stored the veterinarian-prescribed cans that were better for your digestion. Empty. "I'm going to have to go shopping," he grumbled.

But first he headed to the bathroom. Hungry, you followed him. There, he spotted the leftover hair dye. Then he eyed you.

Your pale ginger fur glistened in the sun. He scanned the label. "Pet safe," he read aloud. Mutant scooped you up and shook the bottle.

You could feel the wet streak down the middle of your back. You didn't like the smell. Once it dried, though, it didn't bother you. After he left for the pet supply store, you sauntered past the full-length mirror in Mutant's bedroom. The arch of your back shone with a bright green mohawk stripe, like a badass skunk. You always knew that your pet parent had a counter-cultural bent. Finally, you fit his aesthetic vibe too. Meow on.

Smellyman

"The name that no human research can discover—
But THE CAT HIMSELF KNOWS, and will never confess.
When you notice a cat in profound meditation,
The reason, I tell you, is always the same:
His mind engaged in a rapt contemplation
Of the thought, of the thought, of the thought of his name:
His ineffable effable
Effanineffable
Deep and inscrutable singular Name."

—T.S. Eliot, Old Possum's Book of Practical Cat Quotes

"Two-Legs Dad named me Solomon. So why does Mama call me Smellyman?" my ginger brother asks, whiskers twitching like startled birds.

He yawns like it doesn't matter, but I know better. The sight of Mama makes him slow-blink. He lets her rub his belly without unleashing the hind-kicks of death. Yesterday, he drooled on her hand.

"Names again?" I sigh. "Mama singsongs Smellyman like it's her favorite treat, doesn't she?"

I sniff the plume of his orange tail—damp and wild, like a fox after rain. He bats me lazily, unbothered. I remind myself I'm the

alpha. Yet Two-Legs gives us the same amount of food. Same time, same sized dish. *Outrageous.*

A morsel of sun must have entered his brain. Without warning, he launches into a tail-chase under the eating table. Round and round. Doesn't he know that it's his own appendage?

I've heard Two-Legs Dad say ginger cats share one brain cell. Guess it's not Smellyman's turn.

I pounce, halting his nonsense. We tumble together—his belly a soft drum against my ribs, his back claws half-sheathed. My nose ends up far too close to his pungent end.

"Aww, how cute!" Two-Legs Mama coos, pointing her glowing hand extension at us. She loves that pose. I should teach her some proper cat fight moves.

Smellyman wriggles free. I chase him past the fireplace, our paws skittering on the smooth floor. We dart faster than birds in flight. My heart races, tail high.

What are we doing here? I want to ask.

Playing, he calls over his shoulder.

Not the playing. What's our *job* here?

We crash into the white wall, bounce off, sprint again. I finally pin him down. We're panting. Bellies full of midday meal. The question lingers.

Everyone else seems to have a purpose. Two-Legs Dad rides the roaring grass-muncher. Two-Legs Mama flips tree-pages or taps on her glowing screen. Even birds know how to fly.

Smellyman wiggles away. "I'll show you," he says, padding toward Mama on the sofa.

She sits curled like a loaf, her eyes heavy. The sad wrinkle between them is back—the same one she wore when she burned dinner and scraped black veggies into the compost. Now, her glowing hand shows the younger Two-Legs. "I miss my college boys," she sighs.

Smellyman climbs onto her legs and looks up with peepers as big as a doe's. When their eyes meet, he collapses with love. Accustomed to his reaction, she catches his furry form puddled onto her lap, and laughs. "Are you Goldie?" she whispers, abandoning the screen. Her arms curl around him. He purrs as she strokes the spot between his eyes, not minding that she's called him a different name. Her sad melts away.

"I love you," she says. He drools, one clear drop sliding down his chin. She looks at me. "Love you too, sweetie."

My chest goes gooey. Maybe that's the answer.

My head drops to my paws. My pulse slows.

We are love.

We don't need jobs.

We don't need perfect names.

We just need to *be*.

Maybe Smellyman captured the shared brain cell today after all.

Dear Mr. Melody

Your hello emerges like a snarl.

You approach me on the dance floor, panache oozing from every leopard-print boot stomp, timed to The Prodigy's growling vocals. I twirl in response and sway to the frenetic beat, one arm overhead painting an invisible Sistine Chapel. Pink and green neon lights pulsate over the trim fit of your mesh shirt, red vest, and tartan pants, all cinched with a metal-studded belt and festooned with chains. Your sideways glance acknowledges me. You amp up your moves, a magical elixir of arm swirls, heel thumps, your whole being interpreting and augmenting the music that surrounds us.

In real life, we would probably never cross paths. You'd be unlikely to guess my day job from my zippered black minidress, graced with bondage straps, finished off by combat boots pierced with silver O-rings. I try to imagine where you spend the hours of your life, with your hair spiked in the middle, ear lobes stretched from years of heavy jewelry, exuding enough intensity that one glance could fell an ox.

During tonight's annual event, we gather with those who fondly recreate the dance vibe of The Melody. It's been more than two decades since this nightlife institution near Rutgers University closed. Each year, a handful of the club's celebrated disc jockeys return, DJs who spun for college station WRSU, and one of the first alternative rock stations, WHTG. They pore over set lists and show up early to set up memorabilia. What do you think of the original Melody sign in its decidedly cheerful font and primary colors, as if it's advertising a circus, not a night club?

The Elks Club where the annual gathering had been held for years is being demolished and rebuilt, so for the first time, the reunion is rehomed to a new venue: The Kefi Ballroom. Off a side street in downtown New Brunswick, DJs play alternative rock, goth, industrial, New Wave, and post punk tunes favored by its patrons. It's a welcome time warp.

To the uninitiated, we appear to be an unlikely gathering. Under a disco ball, the haunting melodies of Depeche Mode, Echo and the Bunnymen, or Siouxsie and the Banshees wail all around us. Cocktails are being stirred at the bar. Time (and the dim lighting) deepens the crowd's cool factor. Perhaps sparked by the freedom of our seminal years at the club, each of us seems to have become more ourselves. The eclectic posse includes a lead singer who belts out tunes at live venues, tech professionals who spin music, and a guy whose backwards baseball cap belies his '80s dance moves.

Our artist friend greets friends in a flowing black outfit. We maintain a foot or two of distance from her when we lean in for a hello, respectful not to disturb the fingernails that she's been growing since her teenage years. Her self-dubbed "talons" were featured in *Ripley's Believe It or Not.* They swoop in gentle curves of iridescent purple and blue past her knees, living art swaying to the beat of Joy Division. Her reverence for the venue is forever captured in her iconic illustrations of the original Melody.

©2015 Lauren Curtis

In the middle of the dance floor, the event's originator bounces to the music in the same motorcycle combat boots he's been gracing since 1987, a red handkerchief in his back pocket. The kerchief may appear to be a design choice but turns out to be a functional accessory when hours of dancing turn sweaty. Mr. Melody, I recently learned why our annual gathering takes place in February: for the joy of flinging our steamy dance bodies into the winter air. *Brilliant.*

By day, we are professionals, workers, and retirees. During our reunion, we are all by varying measures reliving our youth. One woman closes her eyes, head nodding to the song's rhythm, as if lost back in 2001, when the original club was last open.

For regulars like us, The Melody represents more than an underground club. Back in the day, when you passed the scrutiny of the bouncer, tucked away your borrowed ID, and flung open the

wooden door, you were *free*. Against a backdrop of neon murals, shouting over a drumming bass, fists punching the air, each of us was freer than we'd ever been. Some to cross-dress, some to chain smoke, and everyone to dance to the song of their soul. Sometimes, an elderly man occupied a corner table, pencil in hand, sketching the colorful characters prancing on our own invisible cat walks. Totally fair. We celebrated ebullience. We encouraged experimentation. We embraced everything except the ordinary.

You know all of this, Mr. Melody, don't you? For me, you embody that time capsule of a period. The reunion marks the years passing–alongside our children's milestones, work advancements, anniversaries, and sadly, the passing of longtime clubgoers and a beloved bouncer. I think of Eric whenever I hear a certain Fine Young Cannibals song.

Like a metronome, The Melody reunion measures the decades since attending college, the time when innocence began to morph into wisdom. I wouldn't trade that wisdom, and yet I still yearn for and love the naivete of those youthful days. Sundays and Wednesdays were quintessential Melody nights, our portal into an emerging subculture, packed with diehard dance fans and obscure tunes until the two a.m. closing time. Were you there the evening when legendary DJ Matt Pinfield (of MTV fame) chucked a rolled-up T-shirt at me? Too busy thrashing to the propulsive beat, I didn't initially realize that I had won the Nitzer Ebb dance contest.

Mr. Melody, did we shimmy to The Cure and stomp to Sisters of Mercy beside each other? No matter how many months pass between The Melody get-togethers, dancing with abandon to hardcore industrial rock will always feel like part of my essential essence.

Your snarl is woven into that tartan fabric, studs and all.

MEETING MY HEROES, true stories

Marcel Proust once warned that we should never meet our heroes—because we're bound to be disappointed. I've met mine. And Proust was wrong.

Essay No. 1: Doc Jacobs

During the publication of my debut novel, my publisher introduced me to Navy Corpsman Daniel "Doc" Jacobs. I had the honor of meeting him and learning about his story.

Doc Jacobs was just eighteen when the events of 9/11 stirred something ancient and unshakable in him: a sense of duty that ran deep through his family's military lineage. He answered the call by training as a Navy medic. In 2006, six months into his first deployment in Iraq, he volunteered for a mission that would forever alter the course of his life.

An improvised explosive device exploded beneath his convoy. In those chaotic moments after the blast, Doc radioed his command: "We've been hit. I can't feel my legs." But where others might have waited for help, Doc moved. His training took over. He tied tourniquets around his own limbs, unaware that the bomb had not only severed his left leg but also broken his neck and back, shattered his forearm, and mangled his hands.

Even in unimaginable pain, he insisted on being propped up, so he could treat the wounded around him. For these selfless actions, he was awarded the Bronze Star with Valor and the Purple Heart. But medals can only partially measure what he did next: he grieved. Two men didn't survive the attack, and Doc never forgot. "Not a day goes by that I don't think of you two heroic souls," he says. "Semper fi."

Doc went on to make history. He became the Navy's first amputee corpsman—and the first amputee in the entire US Navy to return to a deployable infantry unit. When metal in his jaw prevented further deployment, he retired, only to rewrite the meaning of resilience in civilian life. He hand-cycled the 2007 Miami Marathon. Ran the Detroit Half on a prosthetic leg. Tried out for pro baseball. Competed in over 30 endurance races. And always, he wants to serve others. For example, by raising awareness and funding for clean water in East Africa, and founding the Doc Jacobs Foundation to support

military families and kids in sports. His hometown of San Diego celebrates "Doc Jacobs Day" on November 17th.

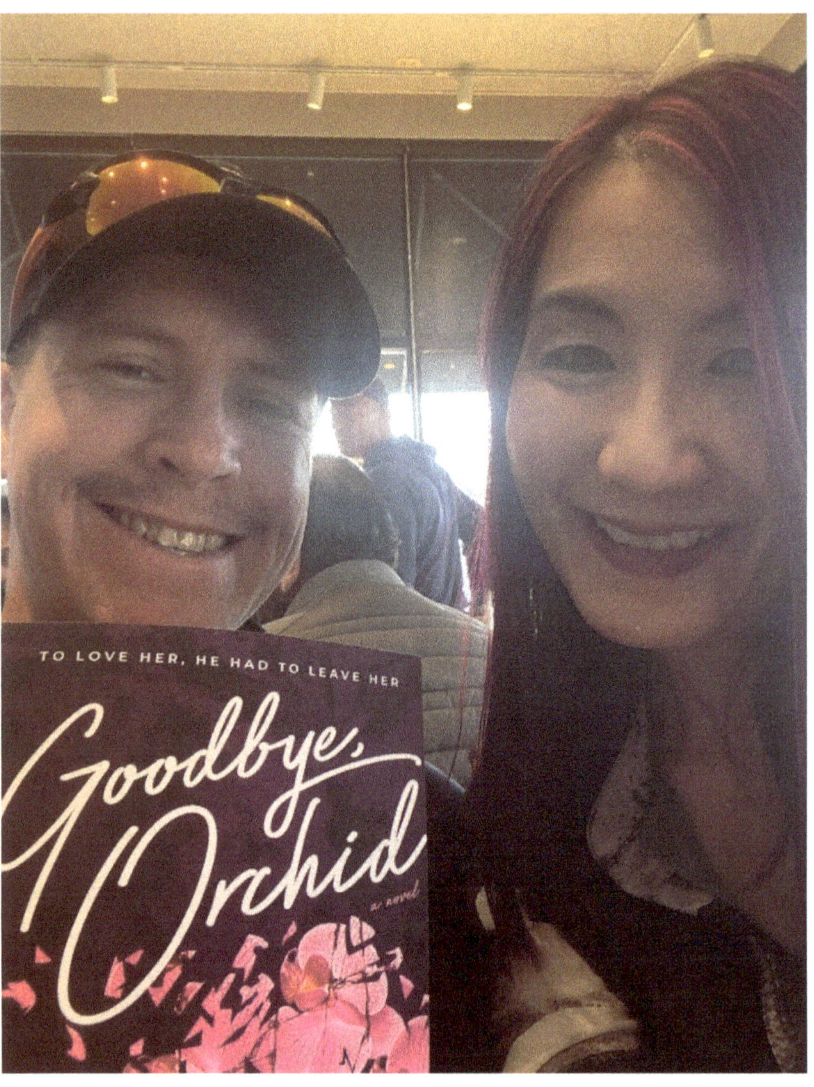

When we met, it was for research on my *Goodbye, Orchid* series. Doc gave generously of his time, allowing me to ask anything. He shared not only war stories, but the quiet, human truths that come afterward. He told me how the novel's multiple points of view—especially

Phoenix's mom, brother, and friends—deepened his own empathy. For the first time, he considered what it must have felt like for his father and "G-ma," who stayed by his hospital bed during his long recovery. That insight moved me—and reinforced my commitment to weaving complexity and compassion into every character.

Even after nearly 100 surgeries over two decades, Doc's challenges haven't ended. A few years ago, his right ankle deteriorated beyond saving. In November 2022, he woke from surgery and posted a photo of his bandaged limb with just five words: "No more legs for me." And yet, he set a new goal.

In 2024, Doc competed for the U.S. Paralympics team—not for sympathy, but for speed. He is now representing his country again, this time on the U.S. Bobsled team.

No more legs. But boundless grit. Overflowing heart. And an enduring legacy of courage, humility, and service.

This is why meeting your heroes can be reckless. Because sometimes, they change the way you see the world—and the way you write it.

Essay No. 2: Noah Galloway

> While my literary agent was submitting my debut manuscript to publishing houses, I became mesmerized by Sgt. Noah Galloway's performance on the television show *Dancing with the Stars*.

During the uncertain months when my literary agent was submitting my debut manuscript to publishers, I found solace—and a surprising kind of courage—in an unlikely place: the celebrity reality show *Dancing with the Stars*. I remember being mesmerized by Sgt. Noah Galloway's performance. Night after night, he moved across the stage with an elegance that defied expectation. But it wasn't just his physicality that captured me. It was his story.

Noah had enlisted in the military after 9/11, driven by a deep love of his country. On his second deployment to Iraq, his Humvee struck an improvised explosive device. The blast changed everything. When he awoke in a hospital bed, groggy and unable to speak—his jaw wired shut—his mother stood at his side, delivering unthinkable news. He had lost his left arm above the elbow, and his left leg above the knee. The explosion had shattered his body. Unable to respond, he could only weep.

In his memoir *Living with No Excuses*, Noah describes the darkness that followed: the spiral into addiction, the loss of purpose. But a prosthetist nudged him toward something familiar, fitness. Through grueling effort and self-discipline, Noah reclaimed his body and his life. He became a competitive athlete, racing in Spartan, CrossFit, and Tough Mudder events. He launched the No Excuses foundation for underserved youth. He inspired millions on *The Today Show*, *Ellen*, and the cover of *Men's Health*, which named him its first-ever Ultimate Guy.

By the time he took the stage on *Dancing with the Stars* for Season 20, he was in peak condition. But the rehearsals were brutal. He and his partner, Sharna Burgess, had to work harder than their peers

to choreograph movements that felt seamless. During one practice session, she accidentally knocked out one of Noah's front teeth. And yet, when the music played, they moved together as if weightless. His prosthesis—once a symbol of loss—now seemed to extend his reach, not limit it.

Watching Noah perform, I imagined my protagonist Phoenix, a man remade by trauma, learning to move again—not just physically, but emotionally, spiritually. Noah's resilience infused my writing. His strength gave shape to Phoenix's arc. That sense of optimism, of grace under hardship, became the heartbeat of my novel.

What I could never have predicted is how Noah's story would circle back to mine.

On July 4th—America's birthday, during Disability Pride Month—Noah reached out to share his thoughts on *Always Orchid*, the final installment in my trilogy. He wrote that it represented "the strength of the human spirit, and the unbreakable bond that can withstand any obstacle." I blinked back tears reading those words. Because to me, *he* embodies that spirit.

His words now live inside every copy of *Always Orchid*, tucked among the testimonials. A special hardcover edition bears his quote on the front cover—my quiet tribute to a man who dances through adversity with power, purpose, and humanity.

It was an honor to send him a signed copy. And today, Noah continues to amaze me—not just as a soldier or athlete, but as a father, husband, speaker, and relentless source of hope.

Proust warned us not to meet our heroes. But I did. And I'm better for it.

Essay No. 3: Bryan Anderson

> This is why meeting your heroes is reckless: because they just might change you. I took that risk when I met Bryan Anderson during my research for the *Goodbye, Orchid* series, and I count myself lucky for it. He welcomed my curiosity with remarkable generosity, giving me free rein to ask anything, and offering more than I ever expected. Time spent with him didn't just inform my writing—it left a lasting imprint on me.

Bryan Anderson's pull towards adventure began with the question, "*What else does the world have in store for me?*" Ever since high school graduation, he'd been hefting luggage into American Airlines airplanes. He wondered, "Is drinking after work with colleagues enough of a life?" His twin brother seemed to be finding his path in a family business repairing heating and ventilation systems.

Seeking adventure, he enlisted in the U.S. Army. His ship-out date? September 11th, 2001. The night his plane left American soil for his first tour of duty in Iraq, Bryan looked out the window onto a flat black sky. Full of conviction, he knew that he would either return home having protected his country or give his life doing so. He never considered that there could be an outcome halfway between those options.

Bryan served for four years, working as a military policeman. During his final mission, he drove his Humvee through the dusty outskirts of Baghdad. His vehicle was the third and final truck in a caravan. Unbeknownst to him, an Iraqi laser beam invisibly pierced the span of the road, set to detonate an improvised explosive device when triggered five times. The first two cars interrupted the beam four times, one for each axle. His commander and second accompanying car passed through unscathed. Then, just as Bryan lit a cigarette, his truck rolled through at a miserly 5 mph and broke the beam a fifth time. BOOM.

An explosion deafened his hearing. Smoke and dust clouded his vision. He was slammed against his driver's seat but didn't sense the damage that the molten metal had wrought on him. Disoriented, he shouted for his men, checking to see if they were okay. He didn't know it at that moment, but they had disembarked, mostly unharmed. What Bryan realized was that he couldn't get himself out of the vehicle. No matter how hard he tried, his legs didn't seem to work.

Hopeful, he spotted two of his friends, Kenny and Michael Wait, outside his Humvee as they unbolted the driver's door to free him. Once they reached him, Michael stared at Bryan and froze. His jaw unhinged; his expression dumbfounded. Kenny gave Wait a shove and shouted "Just go! We'll think about it later!" Shaken out of his stupor, Michael Wait dragged Bryan down onto the hard sidewalk. Then his two friends ran to another vehicle for supplies.

You might think that in the gravest moment of someone's life, angels would flutter down to whisper soft reassurances into Bryan's ringing ears. Or at least he'd be granted a reprieve from mundane concerns. But the universe is not fair. The metallic scent of Bryan's raw wounds attracted flies. He lifted his arm to sweep the swarm away. That's when he caught the first glimpse of his injuries. His right hand was a mass of oozing muscle, ligaments, and jagged bone. It looked like a supermarket package of ground meat.

Before he could fully absorb this new reality, something else interrupted his attention. A fat horsefly landed onto his eye. Instinctively, he blinked and swatted at the pest with his left arm. Except he whiffed air. He gaped at the blank space where his left hand had been for the twenty-four years of his life. In its place, the tattered fabric of his empty sleeve shone scarlet. There wasn't time to fully grasp the extent of the damage. His friends had sprinted back. With a tourniquet kit in hand, Wait dropped to Bryan's side.

Kenny's face was pale. Michael fumbled with the fabric strips. Bryan was injured but surely his buddies had seen worse. *Why were his friends losing their cool?* He lifted his head to make sense of their panic.

Wait tried to push his forehead down.

What doesn't he want me to see?

It was too late. Bryan caught a flash of the carnage that the bomb had dealt. There was nothing where his legs should have been. Just. Empty space. Dusty asphalt. The crimson wetness on his shredded pants wept a story of that dry day in the desert. In a place where vitriol ran so deep that it felt like justification for one man forever shattering another man's life.

As Bryan's head fell back onto the dirty pavement, a thought ran through his mind. *Well things are gonna be a little different from here on.* He had lost so much. Too much for a person to take in. In an instant, the force of the IED's explosion had amputated both of Bryan's legs and his left hand. Another person might have fallen apart or grown hysterical. In his most dire moment, could he rely on the one thing that had accompanied him into adulthood?

Bryan hoped that one part of his essence was still intact. His humor couldn't abandon him. Not in this moment. With his one remaining hand, he grabbed his buddy's arm. They locked gazes. His friend's eyes were crazed, rotating wildly, as he floundered with the fabric of the tourniquets. Bryan could sense the worry lines of his forehead creased up to his hairline.

"Dude," Bryan gasped, every word a fight for air. He would later learn that the explosion had collapsed one of his lungs. His friend leaned closer to hear him, his tight jaw looking as anxious as if he were about to witness a dying man's final request. Bryan didn't have last words of wisdom to impart. He asked the pressing question on his mind. "Do you think I'll ever get laid again?"

After a pause, their laughter broke the tension. With a renewed sense of purpose, his friend fashioned the knots that would stem Bryan's bleeding and save his life. In that critical moment, Bryan's joke saved them both.

Seven days later, Bryan woke to a familiar face peering down on his bed. "Mom?" Bryan's voice rose in incredulity. Whose terrible judgment decided to risk flying his mother to a war zone?

She quickly calmed him, explaining that he'd been in a coma since being airlifted to a Baghdad hospital and then to Walter Reed Medical Center in Washington DC.

"I'm in the U.S.?" His relief burst out in a guffaw.

Then, her lips downturned. She asked if he knew that he'd been injured.

"Yes," he responded, recalling all that he had left on that dusty Iraqi street.

She pressed on. Before he was even ready for rehab, she asked, "You know you have basically two options here, right?"

"Yup, move on or roll over and die," he responded.

He was surprised his mom even needed to ask which option he'd choose.

"I'm moving on," he said.

In the ensuing months, Bryan learned adaptations for everyday tasks and achieved his goals, like greeting his Army buddies for the first time since the blast standing upright and learning to live independently. Since that time, he's built a full and rich life. He's a spokesperson for Quantum Rehab, Gary Sinise Foundation, and USA Cares, a motivational speaker, author, an actor who's been featured on TV shows like *CSI:NY* and movies like *American Sniper.* He competes in a full-contact wheelchair sport whose intensity causes it to be dubbed "murderball."

When we're together, Bryan admits that he wishes others wouldn't judge his life based on his visible disabilities. His daily adaptations don't pain him as much as the things people say. In his memoir, he says: "Even if I could, I wouldn't change what happened to me, because it's made me stronger."

Photo courtesy of Sgt. Bryan Anderson 2023

In my debut novel *Goodbye, Orchid*, my aim was to shed light on injuries like those that soldiers may suffer during active combat. This empathy for others began in my childhood. In pre-school, our class of three-year-olds welcomed a new child. Except she was younger,

only two, and hadn't fully potty trained. *Eww*, an older boy snickered, wrinkling his nose at the white diaper that ballooned out from her shorts. I took in her crestfallen expression.

"Let me show you the sandbox," I said, and led her over to another corner of the playground.

This early lesson on the power of empathy helped fuel my desire to right unfair judgments.

During *Goodbye, Orchid*'s culminating scene, at a friend's wedding, an acquaintance thoughtlessly makes main character Phoenix's accident sound impossibly dire, "You are so amazing, to go through all that. I can't even imagine. *I would've just died*." His love, Orchid, stands up to the acquaintance, stating "I guess some people are just stronger than others."

Sensitivity reader Linda Olson told me how much Orchid's protectiveness touched her. She affirms, "It is comforting to have that protection."

Bryan's story and those of other people with disabilities inspired me with their resilience and reminded me of my childhood friendship with Richard. I imagined a character, Phoenix, who would face life-changing injuries like those that Bryan and other Purple Heart honored veterans had sustained. Phoenix's story would be crafted to inspire hope and optimism for people facing challenges. However, I didn't make him a military character. I placed him into the world of business that I know well from my years working in marketing, strategy, and innovation.

He is named Phoenix since he must rise from ashes. In the story, he meets Orchid Paige who is still dealing with losing her parents in childhood and her resulting PTSD (which is another challenge veterans can face). When a train accident changes Phoenix forever, he's become the very image of trauma that will trigger Orchid. He believes that he's faced with the hardest decision of his life–to protect her, must he leave her without explaining why?

Bryan confirms the angst of this real-life dilemma. When he was recovering at Walter Reed, he didn't want to see his girlfriend but rather wished she would remember him the way he was. Nowadays, both Bryan and Phoenix are just fine with the way they are, demonstrating the human capacity for adaptation.

FATE CHANCE LOVE:
blossoms of fiction

The Orchid family form a dazzling constellation of beauty and complexity, each one a unique whisper of nature's imagination. From blossoms adorned with intricate stripes and delicate spots to those bearing eccentric hairs or warty textures, the orchid defies expectation and delights in contradiction. Some are exquisite; others are strange, even otherworldly—yet all hold an undeniable allure.

What unites this kaleidoscope of floral wonders? In a family so wildly diverse, it seems there are few rules. And yet, among all this variation, one intimate detail remains: a tender fusion of opposites. In orchids, the male and female parts of the flower—the stamen and the pistil—are not separate, but gracefully merged into a single, elegant structure known as the column. It rises from the heart of the bloom like a secret kiss, a symbol of unity, and a botanical act of love that sets orchids apart from all others.

The Orchid Origin Story

No orchid is the same,
each and every orchid
is wild in their own way.

Readers often ask me whether *Goodbye, Orchid* is autobiographical. The answer isn't simple.

My stories are stitched from imagination and research, but the threads of my own life are undeniably there—especially in Orchid Paige, a half-Asian protagonist navigating the intersections of identity, ambition, and loss. Like her, I've built a career in business. Like her, I experienced profound grief at twelve, when I lost my father. And like her, I've straddled cultures, wondering where I truly belong.

Orchid's fashion sense—Dolce & Gabbana, lace and faux fur in spontaneous harmony—is a wink at my own closet. But the deeper reflection lies in her yearning to understand the culture of a mother she's lost, and a homeland she's never fully known.

I know that yearning well.

When I moved to Beijing on a two-year expat assignment, I expected to blend in. My features matched those around me; for once, I thought, I wouldn't be the one who stood out. But my assumptions unraveled quickly.

One evening, over dinner with colleagues at a Lazy Susan table, a friend asked why I was picking up Mandarin faster than other

expatriates. I offered my logic: "Well, they're *waiguoren*, foreigners. I figured people would expect me to speak Chinese."

She paused mid-bite, eyes dancing. "Silly you," she said. "Of course you don't look Chinese."

I was stunned. "What do you mean? I'm 100% Chinese."

She shook her head, pointing at the angled flip of my hair, my black-on-black outfit. "Not with that *toufa*. Not with those clothes." Another colleague jumped in, laughing: "It's the way you move. You're clearly Western."

In that moment, I saw how I'd been carrying an invisible mirror—one that reflected childhood labels, not reality. Back in the States, thoughtless grade school kids had questioned whether I was truly American. In China, I was told I didn't quite look—or seem—Chinese. The irony was inescapable. Those early taunts were wrong. This knowledge freed the truth. I thought that I just needed to find the place where I could fully be myself. Instead, I learned that wholeness isn't linked to a physical location but somewhere deep inside.

That revelation seeped into my fiction. In *Orchid Blooming*, Orchid scrolls through images of Beijing, imagining a city she's never known, searching strangers' faces for traces of her mother. Her journey mirrors my own, the gradual unraveling of mystique and the rediscovery of heritage—not as a fixed identity, but as a bridge between worlds.

Fiction gave me the freedom to re-examine my truths. Writing Orchid's story illuminated my own.

And if there's one truth I return to, again and again, it's this: beneath the surface, we share more than we think. Sometimes, it takes fiction to see that clearly.

Alone in Beijing

Julie Andrews runs through my head. What a mash-up: Chinese American me on spring break in Beijing, dreaming of a story set in wartime Austria.

"The hills are alive with the sound of music," Julie croons in my ears.

Leaves sway in the breeze, their chlorophyll a patchwork of green. Sunshine spills over undulating park grasses. A phrase floats to mind, the voice that accompanies it evokes a touch of pleasure and a shiver of melancholy. "Your head's in the clouds even if your feet are on the ground," whispers the ghost of my mother.

Alone in Beijing's largest park, not another soul in sight, I'm lost as usual. Everyone else is where I'm supposed to be, admiring cherry blossoms. The important thing is that I've made it, all the way from the U.S. to my ancestral country for the first time in my quarter-century on earth. Because my mom wanted me to. Only, we were supposed to visit together. She'd say it was fate. That I was meant to come, even if she's not by my side.

"Things happen for a reason," she'd singsong. When I was young, I ignored her wisdom as ancient fables. I wanted to believe in my ability to control my destiny. Yet here I am in China, just as she'd pictured. Since no one's around, I let my energy out in a spectacularly uncool move. I twirl in my high tops. My flowy blouse flutters over my yoga pants. The unique garment that I scored at the Silk Market features long jagged layers. I imagine floating like a butterfly. It's more likely that I'm giving off the appearance of a lunatic shredded moth. I hum one of Julie Andrews's melodies. I shut out the view of the park and

burst into a running leap. Doesn't she throw her arms into the air like Kate Winslet in Titanic?

Another classic my mom loved springs to mind. "I'm singing in the rain ..."

Oomph. My chest collides into something solid. How did a tree sprout in my path? My feet tangle, tripping over their untied laces. A muscular arm steadies me. I get a mouthful of soft fabric. It smells like fresh laundry, wild with wind. My eyes fly open and I find a clean-shaven jawline, one eyebrow quirked in surprise, shorn hair, and emerald eyes, lined with thick lashes. Full lips are downturned as a blond god studies me.

"Are you okay?" He breathes, then frowns. "*Ni. Hao. Ma.*" His low voice pronounces the greeting like he's repeating a language tutorial. This is probably where he got the tourist phrase that Chinese citizens rarely use.

"*Ni zhemeyang*?" I straighten and attempt to teach him the more casual "how are things going?" that won't sound so formal.

His frown deepens, somehow making his face even more appealing. "*Dui. Bu. Qi.*" He's apologizing, which reminds me that I'm issuing Mandarin lessons from the arms of a stranger.

"*Xie xie*," I thank him for catching me, and extract myself from his embrace. I step back from his warmth and heavenly scent. I see that this tall athlete is clothed in shorts and a tee that stretches across broad shoulders. His searching look is kind. His demeanor makes me feel safe. One strong hand grips an oversized paper.

"A map, thank the stars!" I shout, then feel myself blushing over the old-fashioned phrase that my mom favored.

The furrow between his brows smooths and delight rings out. "You speak English. Thank the stars," he adds dryly. His voice timbers deep and gravelly.

I envisage the way I must look to him, my smooth Asian features, button nose, and thick black hair shot through with electric purple, dressed like a haphazard moth who's flown a mission through fan blades.

"Well, of course, if you overlook the Jersey in my accent."

"Jersey! I'm from New York."

"As long as you don't lord it over me."

"Upstate. Not the city. I have nothing to lord," he assures me. His stance, feet wide, is at once proud and humble.

"Oh! Where?" A piece of home seems to emanate from the cut of his shoulders, the combed cotton of his tee, pale hair trimmed close.

He places his small-town childhood in Rockland County. Not so different than my suburban upbringing, where mom volunteered in the school cafeteria so she could catch glimpses of me chowing down on cardboard masquerading as pizza. This oak of a man and I lose ourselves comparing places and people, when I notice his forgotten park diagram nodding in the breeze.

"Right, the map! I'm totally lost," I admit, trusting this stranger who feels more familiar than anyone or anything I've encountered in this foreign city.

"I'm not sure where we are either. My cell service is really spotty here."

"My battery died. Forgot my charger," I say, holding up my phone as evidence.

"I was coming to ask you if you could read this–"

"When I ran into you."

"More like slammed."

"I didn't see anyone around."

"I was sitting by the tree over there. When I saw you dancing like ... Shakira?" One side of his mouth twitches with mirth.

Heat rises across my cheeks. "Julie Andrews. Tell me this park isn't like the Sound of Music."

His handsome face swivels to peer at the manicured expanse. Humor plays across his lips. "No snow-caps. No mountains. No orphans."

"Don't you see the trees? The blue sky? There weren't even orphans in the movie. But if you need one..." I jab a thumb towards my sternum.

It's too soon. My eyes water. Damn the self-pity. She was meant to be here. This is her dream, not mine. It's so unfair.

The kindness in his eyes holds sympathy. "You okay?"

I jut out my chin. "Yeah, I'm okay. Even if you burst my bubble. I'm sticking with the Sound of Music. Until I can find the cherry blossoms. Then I'll switch to Crazy Rich Asians."

"You're looking for cherry blossoms?"

"Yes, like everyone else."

"How could you miss them? There were signs everywhere by the front entrance."

"I must've come in through a different gate. How about you? If you saw the signs, why aren't you there?"

"I'm not a fan of crowds. I'm here for a run and now I'm looking for first aid." He waves his free hand downwards.

A series of scrapes surrounds a deep laceration on his right knee. Blood oozes down one muscular shin.

"Oh. That's a nasty gash."

"Nah. It's just frustrating. On the last day of my leave."

Leave? Last day? There will be time for questions later. His wound needs attention. I'm not abandoning this guy, with his barely passable "*ni hao ma's*," to find medical treatment by himself.

"Do you want to sit here while I get help, or..."

"I can walk. Let's go together."

"But we're still lost." I lift one edge of the colored paper and together, we study the squiggly lines. The park is shaped like Missouri where I used to attend summer camp. Mom used to send me weekly care packages and would sneak in contraband butterscotch brownies.

"Can you read Chinese characters?" he asks.

I shoot him a sour look. "I only play a Chinese person on TV," I joke.

"Very funny."

"Now I wish I'd paid attention during Mandarin class."

This tree of a man tilts his head to take in the sky. His presence expands like the heavens would bend to his will. "Now that it's late afternoon, I can see where the sun is heading. The south gate must be this way." His free hand indicates the downhill direction. He closes the map, expertly folding the crisp edges together and tucking it into one pocket.

"Gate. Fate. Wait." I singsong, happy for a goal.

"Waite," his voice upturns in a query and he stops.

I pause my gait and glance down, confused if he needs a break. His shin looks the same. "You okay?"

"Yeah." He slides a sideways glance at me. "My buddy's name was Waite."

"Was?" My voice softens. I intuit what the sadness in his tone means. Like he's trying to get away from my pity, he starts down the path again. The sun warms our backs. His shadow looms tall next to my slender one, bobbing along beside him. The wisps of fabric at my side appear to be dozens of butterflies nodding their wings in agreement.

Minutes pass, then he starts talking as if we've been conversing all along.

"Yeah, he was a Marine, like me. Killed in a freak accident, during some routine training. On our base, in South Korea." He stalks down the winding path as if headed to a base just ahead of us.

"Oh, I'm sorry." Marine ... one piece of this man's mystery revealed.

"Thank you."

The terrain begins climbing uphill now. Our walk slows, both of us lost in thought. A warm breeze caresses my cheeks. After a beat, he glances at me and continues. My silence does that to people, draws them out. "We were supposed to travel on leave together. Visit Beijing. After the accident, I was going to cancel. Then my platoon leader thought I should take some time off anyway. So, I came by myself to see the place for the both of us."

I study the groove between his eyebrows. They're etched in pain that seems more existential than physical. I search for some way to comfort him. "That's really thoughtful. I bet he'd appreciate that. Where do you plan to visit?"

"At this rate, a minute clinic would do, and I'd call it a day." I realize that his limp has become more pronounced.

Rivulets of red streak his lower leg, staining his sock and shoe crimson. A single line of ochre footprints march behind us, an imprint for every piece of the puzzle that makes up this enigma of a man.

"Holy hell, that must hurt." I place a hand on his forearm to pause our progress. He's solid, and warm.

"I'm okay. I have a high tolerance for pain."

"Could be, but you need your blood on the inside. Because I definitely can't carry you if it comes to that."

"Believe me, I've suffered worse."

"Hang on. I have an idea." I tug at the longest butterfly wing on my blouse. The fabric sounds with a satisfying rip as it tears from the seam. One hand aloft, my lips stretch across my face with pride.

He presses his mouth together in a failed attempt to dam his laughter. "Fashion show?" he guesses.

"No, silly. Hold still," I kneel on the bumpy pavement and wrap the gauzy fabric just below his knee. Fair blond tendrils wave down below his abrasion. One firm calf flinches as I bandage his wound. My stomach knots in sympathy. "Sorry. Is that too tight?"

His eyes close for a moment and he releases a long, slow breath.

"No actually that's great. Are you in medicine?"

"Funny enough, I did consider med school. But then I fell in love with astrophysics."

"You're smart." Not a question, just a statement.

I peer up at him. The crevice between his eyebrows is shaped like a tiny question mark, as if it's churning over an unsolvable proof.

I'm the only soul accompanying him in this park. He's the only American hero I know. Period. I'm moved by some unspoken bond. Something bigger than I can grasp in this moment. His gaze searches mine.

"Thank you, umm..." He pauses, and I fill in the blank.

"Samantha. I'm Sam."

He takes my outstretched palm in his callused one and helps me to my feet. Sparks course through every capillary, electrifying me to my fingertips. His green eyes, moss-deep, crinkle at the outskirts. "Nice to meet you, Sam. I'm Sergeant David Greer. At your service."

"At your service. I may take you up on that." My voice comes out husky, moved by a connection deeper than the origin of our passports. I'm drawn not only to David's striking features, how he strides with purpose, and the kindness in his expression. We share another bond – the wisdom that no one wants to earn – the maturing that comes from losing a loved one.

He runs a hand through his hair, eying me before resuming our journey. His blond follicles wave longer on top, and short around his ears, like they dare not impede his finely honed senses.

Our path curves upwards. Branches scrape against the blue sky.

"What happened anyway?" I wave towards him.

"To Waite? My leg? Julie Andrews?" He glances at me for clarification.

"Yes. Start with your leg. And Julie Andrews is mine."

"So possessive," he jokes.

A gnarled tree root nearly upends his balance. Without thinking, I steady a hand under his elbow. We're two Americans lost in a foreign land, bonded over a shared familiarity. He reminds me of home.

He rights his stance and talks as we trace the hilly pavement. His long legs are slowed by the injury, which matches my pace. "There's not much to tell. I landed into Beijing Capitol Airport from Seoul a few days ago. They gave me a pass for a long weekend, thinking I could 'blow off some steam.' I spent the evening at the hotel bar last night but it was just so damned lonely without Waite. I figured today a run would clear my head." His voice splinters over his friend's name. Unbidden, I picture a flag-draped coffin next to the plain pine box that my mother chose as a sustainable option. Perhaps my mom was chatting with Waite in the afterlife, welcoming him and showing him the best buffets in heaven.

I continued the conversation, to clear the image from my mind. "So, you came to the park?" I ask.

"I didn't even know where I was going. I had to mime 'run' to the hotel staff." He mimes running which is hysterical even with my butterfly-wing bandage seeping red. "They stuck me in a car and I ended up here. Then I saw all the crowds. I didn't want to be with people. So, I picked all the quieter routes..."

"Until you got lost," I tease this giant.

"Not past tense. We're still lost, if you remember." He tosses me an impish grin.

"At least I stayed upright." Even with the limp, he takes the jab in stride.

"Barely," he tosses back.

"Only because you planted yourself in my path!"

"We're quite the pair, one wounded and one..." He waves at my outfit, no words emerging past his laughter.

"Model?" I finish the thought for him and twirl until my wings flutter. They appear lopsided in my shadow, since I'd donated one long dramatic strand to David's injury.

His diaphragm vacillates between sucking and expelling air, like he's been saving his humor for days.

"These people are going to think you're loopy from loss of blood," I hiss in mock warning, as we start downhill towards an older couple perambulating arm-in-arm. The gentleman tips his hat in greeting. His companion covers her mouth. Our jocularity is contagious.

"I'm a soldier. I don't do loopy. It must be the company I'm keeping." He grins with feigned blame.

A few moments later, he admits, "To be honest, my leg is getting stiff."

One glance confirms that the bandage is no longer ombre gray and white. "What do you need?" I ask.

"Would you take it the wrong way if I leaned on you for support?"

"It depends on which way is wrong," I laugh.

His eyes find mine. The intensity in his contemplation says maybe he means the right side of wrong.

The sun dips a degree. The angle of its rays illuminates a ghost of a sliver down one cheek. A fresh scar.

"C'mere," I offer. Half a step and I'm tucked against his side, one muscular arm wrapped around me. My breath hitches. We nestle like spoons, my yin to his yang. Oh, heaven's scent. Do moths swoon?

"Thank you," he says simply. Relaxing into our rhythmic gait, he asks about me: how I know Chinese, what I'm planning to do in astrophysics, when I'm leaving Beijing. In return, I learn about him, his sister and family, and how the military is paying for his education.

Halfway down the incline, David squeezes my shoulders and points past the trees ahead. "I don't think we're lost anymore."

We round the corner to the sight of impressionistic pink blossoms waving their greetings. I should be relieved. We've found our way. But that means losing our bubble, the two of us on a shared mission. Disappointment sinks in my chest. Our time is nearing an end. *Last day of leave*, echoes in my mind.

I ignore my shadow of sadness. *How ridiculous, we just met.* "It's as pretty as the guidebooks say." I reach for my phone to capture the pale pink petals waving in the breeze then remember my cold dead screen.

David unlocks our embrace and hands me his device. "Go ahead. I can airdrop them to you later."

"Later" conjures images of sharing Mongolian barbeque or laughing over late-night drinks at a rooftop bar. Wishful thinking. Now that we're not lost, nothing would make more sense than to part ways. He has a flight to catch tomorrow.

I take a few shots of branches laden with spun sugar against a blue sky, then turn the lens towards this tall, handsome man. Time ticks, each second closer to goodbye.

"Two fingers up," I instruct, and demonstrate a V with my free hand, the universal photography pose in China. His grin stretches

the thin skin of his scar, then he comes to join my side of the path. I pull up the snap to show him. Instead, he taps the button to turn the camera around.

"Selfie," he says and leans his head down to mine. He smells like clean laundry, with a hint of something masculine. His crescent scar presses against my cheek. Now that I've noticed it, I've memorized the shape of the marred spot in his skin. When the shutter clicks, I marvel how we fit together into the frame as if one of hundreds of shots. Though it's probably the last and only one.

"Enter your contact info if you want me to send you these," he instructs, handing me his phone open to an empty page. I punch in my US cell phone, an email address, and add a flower emoji next to my name. What are the chances that a soldier based in Seoul will remember to forward photos to someone he's met once?

We continue along the path towards the portal. Crowds thicken. We draw closer, as if instinctively protecting the other. David with his hurt leg. Me with my hurt heart. My trip was meant to be with my mom. His with his buddy Waite. Each of us perhaps fulfilling the other's unspoken need.

People swarm around us, a never-ending stream of bobbing dark heads. The air is tinged with the smell of sweat. Tables of wares line the path. Vendors beckon, gesturing at David's height and fair hair.

"Peng you." They shout with palms facing down, fingers waggling us over.

"They're calling you friend," I translate for him.

"Peng you." His voice experiments with the downward slope of the puffed g. Not for the hawkers. The green of his eyes are trained on me. Their hue has deepened in the fading light, as dark as the forest we've left behind.

One woman trails us with an armload of New York T-shirts and black and gold scarves.

"*Bu yao*." I tell her with a wave that indicates we don't want anything.

David captures my hand and elongates our stride, widening our distance from the stubborn saleswoman until her calls grow silent, apparently having turned back. I marvel at the tenderness in his callused grasp.

"Look." I allow one quick squeeze to check if he sees what I see.

"We found our way. Thank the stars," he murmurs my old-fashioned phrase and throws a teasing glance at me. He lets go of our easy hold and checks the back of the map.

The sweetness of meeting this American hero contrasts with the inevitability of the exit now within sight. We're just a subway or car ride from goodbye.

On the other side of the ticket booths, a bustling Beijing city street awaits. Against the evening sky, headlights and gas fumes thrust us back into reality.

David's attention sweeps the concrete expanse, surveying the red columns and park personnel. His military training?

"No phone, no Uber. But I could get you a taxi. Do you want to go to a hospital?" I'm going to look after this American hero the best I can in our last few minutes. My mom would be proud. Head in the clouds even if my feet are on the ground. *Goodbye, David.*

He frowns like he's forgotten about the wound. "I'm okay. Probably just a pharmacy and my hotel will do."

"My phone's still dead so I can't call an Uber but I can tell a driver wherever you want to go."

His green irises pale in the late afternoon sunlight. Spring grasses sway in their impending storm.

"Wherever I want to go?" he repeats.

The space between his brows indent as a question. "Where are you going?"

DAVID

Is she a tourist? Or a sprite? She leaps into the air with joy and my heart betrays me. The thudding hunk of atrial muscle that's wallowed for months. *Traitor*.

She's probably a mirage formed by my unstable mind. I limp from my spot under the shade of a cypress to find out.

Just as I reach the path and flap my map in greeting, she twirls, flinging her arms out like the ballerina inside my sister's childhood jewelry box. Too late, I see that her eyes are closed. Hobbled by my injured knee, I pivot a second too slow to avoid her spinning form. We collide. Her feet stutter. She lists, her cheek landing against my chest. Sweet Jesus she's beautiful. And real.

We wobble, until I right us both. Time stops as I encircle her in my arms, her figure slight like a bird's. Whatever low tune she'd been humming aborts. Her eyes fly open.

The sight of her brown irises swirling with lightning bolts of gold transport me. Back to teenaged summers spent among high meadow grasses, plump bumblebees buzzing, warm rays overhead as I skip rocks across our family's hidden pond. To a time before I'd killed a man.

"Are you okay?" I manage to croak. Her delicate features study me. No fear. Innocence is the only salve to absolve me. *You can't trust me*, I silently warn her.

Does she understand English? I'm not home, no matter that the magic of her gaze makes me feel that I am. "Ni hao ma." I try out the first phrase from my little guidebook. As if 'how are you' can suffice when the time-space continuum has just cracked open.

She responds with something I can't comprehend. Her tone lilts like a songbird assuring baby doe Bambi that all is not lost.

"*Dui bu qi*." I try the phonetic sounds for 'sorry.'

My attempt at Chinese eases the hold that blankets us, and she steps free, saying something unintelligible. This phrase has a soft shh sound that's washed over me at other times in this foreign city.

Her expression unlocks with delight as she catches sight of my map. She's dressed like a fairy from Peter Pan. If I hadn't just held her warm form in my arms, I would've guessed she was an illusory pixie.

Until she exclaims "Map!" like she's won a sweepstakes. No language barrier. I feel mildly foolish for not starting with English. She's even American. Now who's claimed the lottery?

Her chatter as we wind our way towards what I hope is the main gate warms this cooler-than-usual spring day. It thaws a part of me that still can't believe that Waite is gone. It makes me comfortable enough to tell her about my buddy even before we exchange names.

When she bandages my wound from her own clothing, her tenderness almost undoes me. Who is this slender Samaritan? I don't deserve her goodness.

If she's a sign from Waite, he has some sense of humor, sending me this quirky half-angel, half-imp.

We've arrived at the exit before I've unraveled her mystery.

Weakness. Let her go. Nope, I'm too selfish.

"Wherever I want to go? Where are you going?" I ask.

When she says, "Sanlitun," in her light unencumbered voice, I laugh aloud.

"That's where my hotel is too. Share a car with me. If you're heading back, that is."

That's how we end up ensconced in the back of a well-worn Hyundai that reeks of smoke despite the sign which depicts a cigarette crossed out in red. She's so close.

I busy my fingers loosening the knot that's tightened in her makeshift bandage.

"So, wait, you never finished your story. How exactly did you hurt yourself?" she asks.

I pause my motion and lean towards her. She smells sweet, like a garden of roses on a spring day. "Don't laugh."

"Me? Never."

"Well, this squirrel comes out of nowhere and–"

"Squirrel?" Her humor erupts at my expense.

"Yeah, you know, furry brown thing?"

She's holding her side, gulping air. "What'd it do, attack you?"

"No, it runs right in front of my feet. I try to stop, but it gets all tangled up..."

"You tripped on a squirrel?" She can barely get the words out.

"Went right down. The damn thing rolls over and sprints back to its tree like it's perfectly fine."

"Oh, that guy's going to have stories for a lifetime."

"The time he felled a Marine."

The driver crinkles his nose at me in the rear-view mirror.

"Dao le," he says with mirth.

"He says we're here," she explains. It's a relief to have her translate. We're in front of massive wooden doors belted with wrought iron as if to repel invaders. Her stop is first.

Sam cups a hand on my arm before I can form the goodbye that tightens in my throat. "I'm sure they'll have a first aid kit. Do you want to get cleaned up here?"

I look down at the blood scabbed over my knee. "Sure. Dao le." I pay via the app and add a generous tip.

Inside, the wood and glass structure gleams modern and classy. The entrance is scented with citrus. Whimsical chairs shaped like butterflies decorate the high-ceilinged ground floor. The space is both majestic and intimate. Like Sam.

"The Opposite House," she tells me the name of her hotel as she leads me through the lobby.

I laugh. "Perfect for us. Opposites."

"The Marine and the moth," she agrees good-naturedly.

At the concierge's station, she explains our situation and gestures below my shorts. I feel underdressed for this boutique establishment and am glad Sam hasn't seen the bland high-rise where I'm staying.

The hotelier is a well-dressed prim woman who frowns down at the mess of my leg. I toss the makeshift bandage, now reddened, into a nearby waste bin.

"What happened?" She makes polite conversation as she rummages in her desk drawer.

"Killer squirrel," Sam says. Her fingers mime running back and forth.

I cuff Sam on her arm and answer her chuckles with my own. She's buoyed my spirits more times today than I've laughed in the last month. Instrumental hotel music cocoons us, tinkling like a question.

The attendant fills Sam's cupped palms with gauze and slender silver packets. "Why don't you sit in our lobby bar, and I'll have them bring you some clean water and wash cloths?" she offers.

"*Xie xie*," Sam answers.

I hobble beside Sam towards half-empty pods of seating. "What does that mean? I think I heard you say it earlier."

"Thank you," she explains.

We sink into a plush blue sofa, curved around a low circular table. "Well, *xie xie* to you," I say.

When she smiles, white teeth brighten her face. "I bet you would've done the same, a military hero like you."

I feel myself frowning. "I'm no hero."

She pauses her task of laying out the medical supplies on the round surface in front of us. "You know what I mean," she says, trying to decipher what's soured my mood.

A spiky-haired waiter arrives and lays an array of steaming towels, glasses of ice water, two flutes of pale liquid, and a printed paper onto our low table. "Good evening. I'll be your server. The wine spritzers are complimentary. What can I bring you? Perhaps a cocktail?"

Sam sips her aqua and beams at me. "Join me for dinner. Please? Anything you want. On me."

How can I say no to those big brown eyes, rimmed thick with lashes, asking something more than her actual words? Her tumbler aloft, she awaits an answer.

I look up at the wait staff. "Do you serve squirrel?"

Sam nearly spews her drink. He looks confused.

"We'll just take a look at the menu," Sam says, and the poor server leaves.

"You are so bad," she admonishes, clinking her glass onto the marble surface for emphasis.

"You don't even know the half of it," I mutter.

She lifts one moist towel and checks my expression. Obediently, I scooch towards her on the little settee. Scant inches separate us. She applies the compress to my wounded knee, letting the temperate water run down my shin. Her care melts something inside and a prickling behind my eyes surprises me.

"You know I was kidding about being bad, right?" Sam asks softly, catching my gaze.

"Yeah sure. But I'm not kidding," I assure her. A crash sounds from the kitchen behind us, making me jump.

"You okay?" Sam asks. She runs the soft cloth down to my ankle until the fabric comes away red. The blood, the wound, the concern wobbled in Sam's chin, all of it takes me to a different place. I'm on the field. I'm sweating. It's my first time operating this beast of a truck. Waite's trying to calm me. Ah man, it was supposed to be me. Not Waite. Never Waite.

"I can do that." I grab another washcloth and start dabbing at the wound. Its rough surface has cooled and hurts like hell. I deserve worse.

"Hey, talk to me. What's wrong?" Her slender fingers on the back of my hand aren't enough to erase the memories that have unlocked. I may as well tell her. Make her hate me like the rest of my battalion.

"You know what's wrong? You. You are too damned nice." She flinches. Good. She needs to know every ugly detail. I keep going. The floodgates fling open. "You do not even know a jerk when you see one. You want to know what this jerk's done?" I stop scrubbing to poke a thumb into my chest. "I killed a man. Not an enemy. Not in self-defense. My best friend."

Her pink lips fall open. Good. Let her hate me too.

The insidious images seep into view. "It was on a training field. Not even in battle. I'd never driven an armament vehicle this size. Waite said he'd accompany me. He was always there for me. I must've run over something and maybe the gears were already shot. Whatever it was, there was this huge kaboom, and the whole truck rolled over like we'd hit a bomb. When I came to, there was smoke everywhere. And what did I do? Did I remember my buddy? No, I hauled my butt out of there, and sprawled unconscious at the accident site like some selfish jerk." My words grind through gritted teeth.

"And Waite? He didn't get out?" she spoke as if in a trance, like she could picture the whole tragic scene.

"He couldn't. He was unconscious. Knocked out by the explosion. By the time the other guys got to us, he'd been stuck in there too long. They got him to the hospital. But it was too late."

"Oh David. I am so sorry."

"Not as sorry as his parents. He'd just gotten engaged. His life was ahead of him. I am that asshole. It gets worse. I should've gone home for leave. I should've faced his family and told them how damned sorry I am. Instead, like a coward, I came here. I told you, I am no hero."

"It sounds like an accident. Accidents happen."

"All I got from that accident was one stupid cut. Not even a broken bone."

Sam eyes the jagged line. It burns with shame.

"I wouldn't let them stitch it. I turned away the plastic surgeons."

"I don't believe you'd hurt anyone on purpose…"

"Intent doesn't matter. My stupid instinct was to save myself first."

"Maybe it was meant to be. Don't you sometimes think life happens the way it's supposed to?"

My turn to stare at her. "What the hell are you saying? That his number was up, that it was his time? That if I wasn't me being an idiot, he would've died some other way?"

"Why not?"

"Because it was just his random dumb luck to be friends with me."

A tear wells under one brown pupil, then slips over the side, plunging to its demise.

"What?" I ask, my voice soft. My anger dissipates.

Instead of words, tears arrive. Plummeting over her lash line. I close the few inches between us and wrap her in my arms. She buries her face against my chest.

"What's wrong, Sam? I'm sorry..." Oh Christ, now I'm making her cry, this angel who's tried to save me.

She shakes her head. "It's not you."

"It is me. Believe me, it's always me. That's why I enlisted in the first place. To straighten me out."

"It can't be. You're the first person to make me feel better since coming to China."

"How can that be?"

"I came here because my mom wanted me to. We were supposed to come together until she got sick. She made me promise I'd do it anyway. For the two of us. And I thought I'd see her everywhere, that people would look like her, that speaking Chinese would make me feel like home. That's probably why I was thinking about her favorite movie when we met..."

"Killer squirrels and the Sound of Music?"

"No. Lunatic Moth meets Julie Andrews."

Her laughter loosens some of my self-loathing. I feel it floating away like lysosomes clearing out cell refuse. She wipes away her tears. "You see, you're the only person in this country who's made me laugh. Who's made me feel at home."

"I'm the only person you know here, am I right?"

"It's not just that. I wanted there to be some meaning to this trip. Like her dying had some purpose. And you're the only one who's made me feel that way. Like flying seven thousand miles was worth it."

"No. That's you for me, Sam."

Sam's eyes clear and she takes in all of me, from the top of my shorn hair, down to my scruffy unshaven cheeks. Her gaze lingers in the spot that burns down my left cheek.

"Your scar is from what happened, right?"

I nod, not trusting my voice.

She arches up so I feel her warm breath against my neck, and butterfly kisses the rent skin that still burns with shame. Between each kiss, she bestows forgiveness. "You. Sgt David Greer. Are a loyal friend. And a man, of honor."

I fight every proclamation.

Untrue.

Traitor.

Yet her gentle touch soothes a little of the hurt inside.

Lifting the weight of Waite.

She's not running away. I feel her being, so close, almost buzzing with a peaceful energy.

"Your mom loved you. She'd want you to be happy," I say, my mirror a gift to her.

She tries a half-smile. It wobbles along one edge. "Waite would, too," she says, her eyes wet.

The pieces fall together.

I see Waite's bronzed forearm, lifting to high-five me one last time.

"Love you, buddy," Waite's voice rumbles through me. "She's a keeper."

"You're right," I say aloud. And the truth of the words rumble down low in my gut.

She pulls back to smooth a thumb under my eye, slick with wetness. "I'm forever at your service. Even to fight off killer squirrels," she says, her smile a crooked mixture of sorrow and care.

I laugh. It hiccups out like a cry.

She inhales and captures both my hands in hers. "I have a really important question. Promise to tell me the truth."

"The truth is, I hate that shirt."

She smacks my arm. "Be serious."

I lose myself in her liquid gaze. "I've never been more serious."

She looks at me from below thick lashes. "Do you believe in fate?"

Plump bumblebees, meadow grasses, skipping pebbles with abandon. Fate. Waite.

Understanding clicks. My mind names the feeling blossoming in my chest. It's nascent. Yet true. *There's something special about Sam. She's a keeper*. "Do I believe in fate?"

I breathe into Sam's hair, leaning into a space of intimacy. She reaches up, answering my unspoken question, and slips a hand behind my neck. *Roses in spring.* I want to tell her everything. That she's woken something I thought had died with Waite. Faith in another person, and myself.

Our lips meet, soft at first, then they part. A perfect match.

I pause, her beautiful features so close that they're blurry. "You know, I think I do."

We close the infinitesimal space between us, experiencing a plane that is wholly new and yet feels like home.

Some moments aren't about fate.

Some moments, you choose.

Dear Phoenix Walker

Authors interview experts for research. But one literary magazine asks authors to interview their characters. Here is my fictional meeting with main protagonist Phoenix Walker.

Dear Phoenix Walker,

The summer day we meet, the sun has just begun to warm downtown Manhattan's sidewalks. My flowy blouse catches on the wrought iron handle as I push into the flagship Starbucks roastery.

I untangle my clothing. *I'm late. We'll only have a few minutes together.*

You are already inside, sitting at a round table with two café chairs, your blue eyes angled towards your phone. One long leg is anchored to the glistening floor, the other relaxed on the cross-brace of the spare chair. Both thumbs are a blur over your screen, typing a morning missive. Sunlight streams through the windows over your unruly hair and yesterday's stubble, as if you're about to be crowned an angel.

Before I can fluff my humidity-ruined hairdo or cross the vestibule, you raise your eyes from your phone and look pleased to see me approaching. When you stand, your six feet height somehow fills the place, not just this corner of the café, but the whole cavernous space. You abandon your phone and lope over in three bounds.

"Ah, the author herself." You take my proffered hand and we hug hello. I like your spiced cologne and tell you so as we walk towards our table.

"Sorry I'm late, train troubles," I say.

"You're apologizing? Listen, I'm the one who was only available at the crack of dawn."

"True. You must be somethin' to get me here this early on a Sunday."

"Ha. Let me get you a coffee. You still take it black, right?'

"Yep, and yours…let me guess. Double espresso?"

"Best memory this side of the Highline." You nod towards the petite barista behind the counter. She flashes a thumbs up as if there's a pre-arranged agreement. We settle into our seats just as the barista arrives with the exact orders we'd discussed. You had even remembered to request reusable ceramic mugs, in recognition of my sustainability values.

"Thank you," you, the miracle maker, says as she places the correct order in front of each of us. She sashays away with a lighter step that doesn't have to do with her relinquished beverages.

I breathe in the hot brew, relishing the earthy scent as much as the anticipation of caffeine.

"So, how've you been? How are your twins?" you ask, lifting your cup to blow on the steaming liquid.

"You're thoughtful to ask. They're good. I hope they stay as close as you and Caleb."

You set down your drink and study me. "They will. I mean look at all the stuff Caleb and I were able to get past."

"You mean the stolen girlfriends?"

"Ha. Yeah, there's that. Though that was more the symptom than the cause. Looking back, I think it would've helped if we'd gone to different schools earlier. Less comparing. I keep telling him that his tattoo shops are impressive. Especially since Dad isn't here to say that."

"I wanted to say…you know, I'm really sorry about your dad."

"Thanks. I appreciate that. Can't believe it's a year today."

"How's your mom doing?"

"She's okay, she's strong, like all of us Walkers, I guess. I'm seeing her for lunch, after I bring Orchid to the airport."

Your tongue slips softly over the syllables in Orchid's name. One corner of your mouth tugs up. You sip your espresso, lost in contemplation.

Intuition nudges me. I knew that you had planned a vegetarian dinner to celebrate her birthday the night before, but the fiction faeries hadn't downloaded any intel to me yet. I feel lucky to have these few minutes to see you during the magical window just as something is blossoming between you and Orchid. Because I don't know yet what happens next.

"Wait, what's up with Orchid?" I ask. Maybe some new development with Orchid is what prompted my premonition to request time with you. But no, you sound happy and the feeling that led me to contact you was laced with foreboding.

"She's going to Asia to set the beauty industry on fire. She's been working towards this assignment for months."

"Not just her. You two did that together, right? You're the one who gave her the pro bono work for the military non-profit."

"I'm not taking credit for her success. That military ad campaign was sheer brilliance. Sure, I gave her guidance. But she did the hard work. The killer is that with everything she has been through, she feels the pain of those injured veterans as if it were her own. She cared so much, she would've raised a billion bucks for them if she could."

You duck your chin, as if embarrassed over your impassioned speech. You run a thumb along your cup's ceramic rim, seemingly lost in thought.

With a little shake of your head, you refocus on me. "Speaking of Orchid, I'm sorry but I'm going to have to pick her up soon. What else can I help you with?" you ask, not unkindly.

"Oh, nothing in particular. Just, I had this funny feeling. A premonition? I wanted to make sure you were fine. Be careful, okay?"

You flash your perfectly white teeth. "Seriously, I've never been better. What could happen? I'm heading to JFK which I've been to a zillion times. I'm going to work out, then I'm meeting my mom for lunch. If anything, you watch yourself, with those train delays and all."

We stand for a goodbye hug. You toss a twenty onto the table and stride beside me to the door.

"You're going to make her day with that tip."

"I hope so," you say. "It's almost all the cash I have."

"You need some? After all, you didn't have to treat for the coffee," I say, digging for my wallet.

"Oh c'mon. It's my pleasure. Save that for your boys. And thanks for your concern. Don't worry about me. You want a ride to Penn Station?" You push open the door and let me exit first. We step out into the warming day.

"No, there's no need. You don't want to be late for Orchid, right?"

With mention of her name, a smile sneaks onto your cheeks. You glance at the time on your phone. "Yeah, I promised to take her to the airport."

"You take care of yourself, ok?" I repeat, apprehension percolating along the hairs of my upper arms.

You loop an arm around me, unperturbed. "You too," you say. We embrace one more time and you wave goodbye as I turn the opposite direction from where you're heading. Halfway down the block, I glance back one last time to watch your easy gait disappearing around the street corner.

Then I stride towards my train, contemplating the contrast between our light-hearted interaction and the disquiet that echoes inside me.

Your obvious joy should fill me with glee.

I pass a kiosk whose newspapers shout tragic headlines. In New York and beyond, mishaps and ill will result in grief and suffering.

But you and Orchid appear to have everything going for you.

I allow the feeling of your buoyant mirth to blanket me, to quell my unease.

Yes, I just needed to see you.

All seems great.

For now.

Orchid Dear

ORCHID

Orchid feathered her fuchsia lipstick and fluffed her hair an umpteenth time. She couldn't concentrate on the novel that she'd been wanting to read all week. Her phone indicated that they would be late for their dinner date with her best friend and her husband. Trusted babysitters were hard to find and her friends' sitter could only relieve them for two hours tonight. This evening was intended to celebrate Phoenix and Orchid's recent engagement. She hopped off the one-armed settee and took the few strides to their bedroom. The door was ajar.

"How could you possibly take longer than me? I could write a whole brief in the time you've taken!" she said to Phoenix.

She meant her joke about the advertising work that had brought them together to sound teasing, but as she entered the room, Phoenix's eyes had widened, and then he looked down, lips compressed. Her tone had emerged shriller than she'd intended. Her words had cut him.

He was perched on the edge of the bed, his full hair flopped over one eyebrow, a blue button-down shirt exposing his bare chest. One hand had been guiding his pants over his prosthetic leg. He'd paused his motion, absorbing what sounded even to her like a critique.

Orchid realized her error in judgment. He hadn't been preening like a prima donna. He hadn't been dawdling over a Netflix show. Independent, proud Phoenix had been struggling with a daily task that Orchid only found difficult when her multitude of clothing combinations made it hard to choose what to wear.

"Sorry," he mumbled, and stood, seating his residual limb into the socket of his prosthesis. He tugged his waistband over his hips and angled away from her, trying to hide the awkward task of buttoning his pants one-handed.

By the time she closed the distance between them, she could feel the tension between her eyebrows. "Oh honey, it's okay."

It wasn't okay. The hunch of his shoulders confirmed this. He wouldn't meet her gaze as he labored to align each shirt button with its buttonhole. Experience had taught her that offering her help would simply further emasculate his ego. Instead, she tiptoed up to peck his cheek and whispered into one ear. "If we had more time, I'd rather *undress* you," she promised.

He rewarded her with a kiss. The sweet taste of forgiveness couldn't erase her wish to undo her blunder. Still, the evening wasn't a total loss. They were only ten minutes late and even had time to enjoy dessert with their friends before returning home.

That night, though, Orchid slept fitfully. Waking with a start, she picked up her phone to check the time. 2:56 a.m. Phoenix's breathing soothed her, his familiar melody of slow inhales and soft exhales reminded her of their good fortune. She'd finally convinced him that he was still her smart, kind, gorgeous entrepreneur, no matter what he might think he was missing. Tonight's pained expression meant that old wounds lingered.

Frustrated that he could so readily imagine that she was judging him to be lacking, she typed a new phrase into her phone's search bar: "Clothes for amputees." She was part of Phoenix's world now. She would find ways to show him care as he had generously done for her.

After she'd learned about Phoenix's accident that he'd hidden from her, Orchid had schooled herself on what he might need. She had bought him an adaptive cutting board and ensured that their international assignment included an apartment with an accessible bathroom and lowered kitchen sink.

Until tonight, she had not dwelled much on how he got dressed, probably because he always kept their bathroom door shut as he readied himself for the day. In fractions of a second, Google served her videos of amputees sharing techniques on how to get dressed. Ads appeared at the top of the page. The words "Tommy Hilfiger adaptive" caught her eye.

Adaptive clothing? She propped her pillow behind her head, feeling curiosity grow. The page opened to showcase crisp white shirts, casual shorts, soft tees, using magnetic clasps for easy closure. A long-sleeved cotton button-down caught her gaze; its shade of blue would brighten the stormy cobalt of Phoenix's eyes. Had he already tried this line? Would he take it as an affront to his independence? Yet, what better way was there to show that she empathized with his dilemma. That she wouldn't rush him the next time they had plans. Tired now, sleep pulling at her eyelids, she entered his size and checked out.

Three days later, the doorman handed Orchid a package with her name on it. Perfect timing for tonight's dinner date. *Or was it?*

Orchid pushed through the front door and kicked off her shoes. From the other side of the apartment, water drummed against their shower pan. She fingered the ribbon looped around the shirt box and wondered whether she should barge in to see Phoenix or not.

Her gift was meant to express her care.

Except would he take it the wrong way?

How she'd regretted last week's slip-up.

The sound of running water stopped, breaking her reverie and bringing her back to the present moment. She looked down at the Tommy Hilfiger box in her hands, wondering how he'd react to the gift.

It was now or never.

Orchid tossed her purse aside and sailed past their bookshelves. A framed photo of the two of them at the beach before they'd dated showed their laughing faces pressed together, wind whipping their salt-thickened hair.

Ah, what innocence.

Each step towards the bathroom reminded her of their joys and challenges. When they first met, he had agreed to mentor her. Phoenix had provided the ad experience she needed to prove herself to her boss. Then he'd saved a man's life and what he lost made him think that he needed to protect her from him.

She tapped on the bathroom door. "Phoenix?" she asked, her tone lilting up.

"In here, Kai Lan," he called, using the nickname that had stuck when they'd first discussed the children's Mandarin language show.

She pushed the door open to see a razor against the planes of one cheek, his bare chest reflected in the half-steamed bathroom mirror. Once he'd seen the razor as an escape route. He'd promised her that those dark days were behind him.

"I have a gift for you," she sang out, stomach tingling with anticipation.

"It's not even my birthday." His tone playful, he placed the razor at the sink's edge and turned off the streaming water.

She thrust the box towards him before she had remembered that he wouldn't be able to both hold the gift and open it.

He managed the tricky juggle, tucking the bulky item under one elbow and slipping off the bow with the flick of a finger.

She watched him place the box on their counter and dislodge the cover with one thumb. This was perfect. It had to be. Over their time together, he was the thoughtful one who had arranged her Dom Perignon birthday dinner. During their time in China, he had gifted her the amethyst ring that sparkled on her ring finger as a reminder of their shared promise.

Now, he peeled back the tissue paper one sheet at a time, every layer seeming to represent the barriers that had dissolved between them: misassumptions and fears, each one overcome and replaced with trust.

At last, the blue chambray winked up at them. The brilliant azure shone under the recessed lighting as nuanced as the waters of Nice during their visit to Cannes.

He held up the shirt to his bare chest and peered into the mirror.

She sucked a breath. "You look like the model in the catalog."

"Ha. I doubt that they're using one-armed models."

"Well, actually–" she began, watching him unloop the tag from the buttonhole, his struggle mirroring the delicate dance of pride and care in relationships.

Phoenix didn't get it. Not yet.

Then the tag tumbled to their tile floor. The closure opened and snapped shut again.

His mouth fell ajar. He leaned closer to study the shirt.

"What the–" he asked, his mouth downturned.

Oh no, not again. She held her breath. He'd initially resisted the special cutting board she'd gifted him so they could cook together. She reminded herself that he now used it daily, a sign of acceptance, not just of adaptations, but of her help.

He pulled back a button and startled when a magnetic force snapped it back in place.

"They're magnets. They look like buttons, but magnets hold them together," he said, his face relaxing as understanding dawned.

"Ingenious, isn't it?" she asked, a small bit of hopeful pride beginning to warm her insides.

"You're brilliant," he said, as he unsnapped the front buttons and slipped the shirt on. The two sides clacked closed. Together, they looked at the handsome couple in the reflection of the mirror. She hadn't realized that she had subconsciously chosen an aquamarine dress that complemented the pigment on his outfit.

She leaned her head against his shoulder. The image of the two of them in the clearing mirror filled her with elation. "Not me. The designers are brilliant."

He glanced at the box on the floor and turned to wrap his arms around her. "But you're the one who thought of me."

She returned his embrace. He was warm from the shower and smelled of soap and spice. Well-being ballooned inside. They had everything, most of all a hard-earned understanding between them. Love meant having the courage to care, even when you might get it wrong.

"I always do," she said.

He leaned down, his lips finding hers. The rest of her thoughts fluttered from her mind.

No matter. No need for words.

Her arms tightened around his waist beneath the fabric as velvety as the tender interior of a rose petal.

Good humor burbled up through her.

Her dear Phoenix.

Small gestures *can* convey deep emotional resonance.

Love echoes in the details.

RIDDLE: How does a hungry bird begin at the end?

ANSWER: A hungry bird begins at its nest, the soft place where it first learns to feel safe. In the end, if it's lucky, it may find a sacred space that sates not just its hunger but self-acceptance.

Let Us Begin at the End, Hungry Bird

ORCHID

We are officially late.

I imagine our wedding planner's pen scratching out new times for our reception schedule. Yet what can we do? Our photographer posed us for ninety-two painful minutes, fussing over the angle of our embrace to ensure Phoenix's pant cuff covered his prosthetic leg. There was some nuptial ideal in his mind that we just didn't have the chops to pull off. *There is nothing we need to hide*, I wanted to tell him.

We've battled for this day, past star-crossed misconceptions, in sickness and health. I take time to absorb every detail, in order to replay these moments for years to come. The overhead sun glittering in Phoenix's hair. His elbow entwined with mine. I lace his fingers between mine.

My chest expands with hope and enough love for every living being. Today, dressed in a thrifted blush tulle dress, I've accepted a public promise, an offering at an altar. A covenant that billions of people have undertaken, one that indicates how far my trust has rebuilt since my parents' demise twenty years ago. Now, our limo is the pristine opposite of their crushed metal. Robert Smith's vocals

growl on the sound system, in honor of one of the post-punk bands that my parents favored.

Phoenix holds my hand in the back of the car. I marvel at the sensation of his ring threaded between my fingers. He'd once admitted to me that he had grieved not having his left hand to wear his wedding ring.

"It looks good on you," I say.

He studies my simple band that sits beside the purple amethyst promise ring he'd gifted me in China. "Yours too. How are you feeling, Kai Lan?" he asks, his vowels mellifluous over the nickname he'd given me the day we met.

"I'm starving," I say with a laugh.

"Ah, my hungry bird." He releases his hold to pat the breast pocket as if he might find an energy bar tucked inside. He comes up empty.

"I'll eat after our first dance." *After his surprise.*

His mother sits opposite us, as if examining the past while Phoenix and I speed towards the future. "We're almost there," she says. Veronica cranes her neck to point out the window. Her pale silk cardigan twists along with the motion. She remains as solid and poised as ever.

Aunt Betsy and Uncle George's two-story house is just visible. Their elegant home's white siding is polka-dotted with something pink. As we roll closer, I see fuchsia peonies draped over the covered portico, looped through the stair railing, framing the front door.

"You did all this? How did you know?" I ask Veronica, touched by her thoughtfulness.

"Phoenix told me that peonies are your favorite," Veronica says. She had offered to decorate our reception venue, interviewed us for our preferences, and kept this sentimental touch a secret.

"They're my mom's favorite too," I say. Generous blooms decorate the front of the two-story home. In my parents' wedding album, my mother beams in an alabaster gown and my father puffs his chest with the misbelief that nothing could harm them.

"No one can ever replace your mom, dear. But just so you know, you're part of our family now," Veronica says, as if her thinking is on the same path as mine. She's not just Phoenix's mom. Veronica is my *mother-in-law*.

As we near the clapboard home, the familiar steps I'd descended after I'd discovered Phoenix's father's last wish, are gleaming with a new coat of paint. They're freshly white like a clean start.

Phoenix wraps an arm around my bare shoulders. "It's true, Mom. So, you might want to take back the threat that you'd kill her if she hurt me."

Veronica leans forward to pat his knee. "She hasn't hurt you. She healed you."

His lips press the truth of his mom's words into my hairline. Veronica's praise, along with her joy and generosity these last months, thaw a portion of my nerves. The car rumbles to a stop in front of the stately summer home. Anticipation rolls through me. It's almost time to unveil my surprise. Sleek sedans line every visible spot down the beachfront street. Dozens of guests have begun enjoying mimosas and canapes while we finished our group photos.

The driver jogs around and flings open the back door.

The three of us disembark, Phoenix placing a hand under my elbow to help me out of the car. Saltwater scents the air, just as it had the night so many years ago when Phoenix had rejected me in this same house. But on this clear blue-sky day, the salty smell comforts rather than stings.

We stroll along the sidewalk to the house. The sounds of clattering glasses and chattering wedding attendees emanate from the backyard.

Veronica glances at her phone. Time is short. "Twelve minutes until your first dance."

"I am going inside to change," I say.

"I'll go check on the guests," Veronica says with a wave, and stalks through the grass.

Phoenix pushes open the heavy door and allows me to enter first. He points with a flourish towards an entry table filled with family pictures. "Aunt Betsy added this."

I recognize our engagement photo, Phoenix's expression of awe and my left hand lifted aloft.

"That's so thoughtful," I say, picturing the day that we had invited our friends and family to Central Park to celebrate with us.

"We have a lot of memories here," Phoenix says as we pass through the entryway.

"The first place we really talked," I say, remembering my incident with the broken glass and the way that Phoenix tended to my wounds here.

We pass through the airy foyer to a pale blue living room on the left and family room on the right. "You let me clean up the cut on your foot here. I'd fallen for you already by then," he says.

"I didn't want to admit it then, but it's not like I hadn't noticed you either."

"For such smart people, we were slow on the uptake," he says with a chuckle. We pass the sofa and head towards the carpeted stairs.

Halfway down the staircase, Phoenix places a hand on my forearm, staying our motion on the landing. His heat presses into my flesh, with a cool indentation where his ring nestles on his right ring finger. "Enough joking for a sec. I do want to apologize for saying you're worse than the person who caused my accident."

I recall his words hurled up at me before he disappeared down the stairs during that long-ago Easter weekend.

"You were hurt," I say, suddenly seeing the moment of his seeming rejection with a new clarity. "It wasn't as much about me, as it was about what you were going through."

He ducks his chin and accompanies me down the final steps. "It's no excuse. I am sorry."

Another link of empathy softens inside my chest. "Thank you."

"Sounds like you've forgiven me," he says, and leads us into the guest bedroom where I'd eased Phoenix's phantom pain one long-ago night. Two suitcases sit propped open next to the leather chair where I'd stayed that evening. Now, my thrifted dress for tomorrow's brunch lays strewn on the double bed.

"You're forgiven if you're on time for our first dance in ten minutes," I say as I ease the zipper down the back of my dress.

"Deal," he says, kissing me and disappearing into the bathroom.

The feeling of his soft lips lingers as I hang my poufy gown in the closet. Next, I tug on a slender Chinese qipao dress, a nod to my mom's heritage and also a link to the Beijing waitress who'd nearly caused us a misunderstanding. That's all behind us. A sense of joy fills me as I sit in front of the makeup mirror to reapply my mascara.

Before long, Phoenix saunters from the bathroom, hair freshly neatened. His lips stretch wide in happiness, as if there were no other shape for this bright day under a high blue sky.

I dab on lavender-scented lip gloss, from the makeup line I had launched in his honor and stand to join him.

"I see the way to forgiveness is humor," he says.

"There's nothing to forgive between us. Nothing," I say.

His hand in mine, we head out the back door where a hubbub of voices mingles with a tinkle of bubbly jazz. The sun warms my face. In the middle of the oversized tent, each pole wreathed with ivory flowers, the DJ coaxes people onto the dance floor. My feet move to the catchy beat of an '80s pop hit. My heartrate tips up a notch. My surprise for Phoenix is just beyond the DJ stand. "I have something I want to show you," I say.

"Me too," he says.

We step into the shade of the tent and absorb the hum of guests seated at white linen-topped tables situated around a parquet dance floor. The threads of our lives are patchworked into Aunt Betsy and Uncle George's grand backyard. The smell of peonies waft by, reminding me of my rose soap, with a hint of Phoenix's spice.

During the moments we remain incognito, I take in familiar faces. My mom's petite sister Aunt Lily is leaning forward, telling a story to my dad's brother Uncle Zach and his family. She's wearing a peony-print sundress that makes my eyes water. *Just like mom's.* I hope they're replacing memories from the last time they'd seen each other at my parents' funeral with new, happier moments.

Phoenix's Chief of Staff Liv is chatting with my best friend Mandy and her husband, her cat eyeglasses glinting as she gestures. Next to them, my godson Matty is swinging his chubby legs under the table as he disassembles one of the wedding favors. The box's white surface is printed with a repeating pattern of our initials, alternating between "O-P" and "P-O," an inside reference to our joke after Tish's wedding that our initials could either stand for 'opportunity' or as Phoenix teased, 'pissed off.' This afternoon, Matty's joyful presence toddling down the wedding aisle was more the former than the latter. His vigorous lobbing of pink petals had elicited chuckles and clicking shutters.

On the other side of Liv, Phoenix's agency partner Dex is decked out in a plaid bowtie, emerald-green dress shirt and matching suspenders, a more boisterous version of the threads he'd been sporting when we first met at the Effie Awards show. He and his wife Fiona are sitting with wounded veterans Aaron and Tammy.

Aaron touches his beer bottle to Tammy's martini glass. Their faces inclined towards each other. Aaron had checked to see if we minded him wearing Bermuda dress shorts to our ceremony, so that he wouldn't overheat under the summer rays. Now, I see Tammy with a hand on one of his bare prosthetic knees, mouthing something that makes Aaron throw his head back in laughter. They have more in common than their military service. I'm happy that they're together. I sprinkle a wish for unconditional love onto every person in the room.

As we pass the head table at the edge of the temporary parquet dance floor, Veronica motions us over to the spot where she's sitting with Phoenix's brother Caleb. Acknowledging the formal occasion, he has replaced his roughed-up leather jacket with a dark shirt and dark jacket. Peeking under his dress pants are the silver buckles of his Harley-Davidson boots. Beside him is a dark-haired beauty in a red latex dress, Caleb's business partner Sascha. The exes have pushed their chairs close, fingers brushing as Sascha reaches for a sip of his cocktail. When I had arranged for them to sit side-by-side, my romantic heart had hoped for sparks of honest communication between them.

"There you are, missy," Sascha says and stands to kiss me on the cheek. She's beautiful, tasteful ink encircling both arms, pink blooms of blush on each cheek. Caleb takes a swig from his bottle and lifts it towards his brother in a mid-air toast. "I'm giving you sheets for your wedding, in honor of Tish," he says, evoking the name of Phoenix's ex-girlfriend and the present we had gifted her at her long-ago nuptials.

"Don't go stirring trouble," Phoenix says with a laugh. I know that Caleb is joking. Last week, he shipped us an incredibly thoughtful present. I opened the box from him to find a version of the old-fashioned dial phone that I had once admired at his tattoo shop.

Out of the corner of my eye, I spot a swaying figure approach us, a friend who we had met at the Great Wall in China. I wave hello and introduce him to the table. "This is our friend Billy. He drove from Long Island to join us."

"Hey," his words slur. "That is the coolest outfit ever," he says and eyes Sascha's red latex-clothed cleavage, Barbie-doll waistline, and hip-hugging skirt. In my experience, he's a sweet guy who doesn't mean harm. At the moment, though, his thick tongue and steadying hand on the table right next to Sascha's elbow could be misinterpreted.

Caleb slams his bottle onto the table. The surface of a nearby glass of water ripples. He lumbers to his full six and a half feet and sticks out a meaty paw. Billy looks at him, eyes wide, and returns the handshake. "I'm Phoenix's brother Caleb and this woman with the 'cool outfit' is my business partner and the love of my life," Caleb says, his gaze raking over Sascha.

Veronica's mouth falls open. Sascha blinks in surprise, shakes her head once as if clearing her hearing, and then her shoulders soften. My heart soars with hope for Sascha and Caleb. That's the most honest sentence I've heard him utter about their relationship.

"Nice to meet you," Billy says, his nasal tone suddenly sober. "I think I'll refresh my drink." He slips off to one of the nearby bars.

Before anyone else can respond, my boss Joan high steps over and interrupts. "There's the couple I introduced!" I peck her cheek in greeting. No need to correct her notion. After all, she did invite Phoenix to our first work meeting and bring me to counterAgency's anniversary party.

Heads swivel towards our chatter. A high, sweet voice calls out over the din. "They're here!"

Mandy hurries towards us. It must be time. In a bronze dress that matches her blonde highlights, she is every bit my partner-in-crime to unveil Phoenix's surprise. "Come," she calls to Phoenix and takes my elbow, drawing us onto the dance floor.-

As the crowd notices us, spontaneous applause breaks out. Guests clink butter knives to their glasses, chanting with increasing volume. "Kiss! Kiss!"

The DJ starts a new song. The opening bars sound familiar. My toes start tapping. Our friends clear a circle around the spot where we've emerged onto the edge of the wood floor demarcated for dancing. Phoenix leans down to touch lips to the side of my mouth. Hollers of encouragement ring through the open space. Then he leans towards my ear. "Do you remember that you wanted me to take dance class?" he asks over the growing beat of what I now recognize as a Rihanna song.

"Yes, but we decided we didn't need lessons for our first dance. Plus, this isn't the right song. Where's our wedding planner?" I look around for an efficient presence in navy blue to alert the DJ to queue up the correct number.

Mandy reaches us with a chair under one arm. The dance crowd disperses to their seats. “Sit,” she says with authority to me as Phoenix sweeps away.

“Hang on,” I say because this isn’t what we’d discussed. Then my attention is drawn to the center of the dance floor which has otherwise cleared. I sink onto the plush surface.

A spotlight beams. Phoenix stands with the panache that he’d demonstrated at our advertising shoot, back facing me, right arm lifted aloft, fingers snapping, hips keeping time to the beat. His business friend Kit jogs to join him, whom I’d finally met this weekend. He had flown in from China this morning. He is stylish in a slim suit, not jet lagged after his twenty-hour trip. Phoenix’s cousins Harry and Stew bound onto stage, their ties back in place. Dex follows, his bow tie bouncing. Each man mimics Phoenix’s stance, hips swaying, snapping their fingers high in the air. The four of them form a ‘V’ with Phoenix at the center. They begin to turn, one after another like a set of dominos.

“Oh my,” I say as Phoenix is the last to rotate, delight rippling down my abdomen.

Harry and Stew kick into gear on either side of Phoenix. The three of them bust into raucous dance moves, stance wide, kicking side to side, chests pumping to the beat.

A catcall erupts behind me. Probably my coworker Violet, her lavender hair hued to match her pale purple dress. Her admiration is well-founded. Phoenix’s confidence is impossible to ignore. He is no longer simply the Beckham lookalike I had met in a men’s room. His sense of purpose has grown beyond what he could even achieve as Ad Age’s youngest agency founder. He is now CEO of The Walker Institute, innovating to gift amputees prostheses without relying wholly on donations.

My Phoenix has risen from ashes.

My Phoenix, full of benevolence for a man who had cost him limbs.

My Phoenix, who sacrificed to travel with me to China and back.

Phoenix who loves not just me, but himself.

"They're like pros!" My best friend Mandy leans down to shout over the amped up speakers, her camera trained on the five of them.

"You're in on this," I yell back, unable to stop grinning.

Kit swings his arms in time to the chorus, and Dex's shimmy joins in. The crowd cheers.

"Where have you been all my life?" Rihanna's vocals wail.

My hand lifts to cover my mouth. Time rewinds. Phoenix was listening to this song when he saved Roy from the train tracks. He had confessed that he had my playlist on repeat that fateful day in the subway station. Earbuds in, he didn't hear Roy approaching from behind. When Roy rushed towards the speeding train, instinct made Phoenix grab the guy and save his life. Since that day, he has only visited 86th Street Station twice: once upon his brother's request and a second time looking for me.

Rihanna's wail hits a high note. My chest fills with pure elation at the groomsmen's performance. Phoenix notices and hams it up for me, flinging his stance wide. The anthem echoes its final bars. Rihanna concludes that she's "searching for you, babe." Phoenix glides onto his knees and slides to a stop in front of me. The whole room erupts onto their feet. They're shouting and laughing. Mandy runs to the enormous silk sheathing that covers the wall behind the DJ's stand.

I help Phoenix to a standing position. He pulls us together. We're close enough that I want to wipe the sheen of sweat from his face. So, this is love. Expansive and surprising, tingly down to my shins. Thunderous applause vibrates through me. My arms around Phoenix, I feel my hot-roller curls loosen and stream behind me. In my peripheral vision, a pink silk curtain flutters to the ground. Amid his surprise, I take him by the hand and nudge him to view the eight-foot-high wall.

"I hope you like it," I say.

On either side of Mandy and the DJ, an enormous photo stares back at us, one of Phoenix fist-pumping into the air during our advertising shoot. Next to it, Phoenix and I are kissing, the flurry of a gym behind us. The second photo wasn't part of my plan. I scan the room until I spot a head of purple hair bouncing. Violet is clapping and stomping her feet. The extra picture must be her surprise. She had snapped this one of us. The two images are perfect in unison. His ebullient fist-pump lives in context.

Phoenix hugs me to him, studying the larger-than-life images, absorbing us together. "When I was in the hospital, I never thought this could be possible," he says into my ear.

That handful of words brings back memories of the barriers that we've climbed to achieve this moment. Just then, a familiar chord rings through the tent. Our guests' shouts ricochet off the tent and surround us. Hands slap together. The DJ starts up our first dance song and lifts both arms to welcome the crowd. Full of energy, our guests join us. His twin brother Caleb thumps Phoenix's back with congratulations. Aunt Lily comes to kiss my cheek. Soon we're all dancing, bottles aloft in the air, chanting lyrics or making them up.

Phoenix's dove gray suit suddenly takes on new meaning. His Achilles heel had been a pursuit of perfection that is unrealistic. Now, it seems as if his tendency towards black and white, towards an unattainable perfection, is all blended into a soft gray, the color that reflects the multi-layered nature of most things._As for me, twenty years ago, I thought I'd lost my ability to trust in anyone besides me. Now here I am, committed to Phoenix for a lifetime, a new family to call my own. I haven't yet told him about the baby in my dreams from the night before our wedding. I will. Because it's not just Phoenix I trust. I trust myself. That's life. All of us, navigating challenges the best we can, making up lyrics if we need to.

My imagination flashes forward to our honeymoon in Africa and the triathlon that Phoenix has begun training for. Then unbidden, I see Phoenix, temples graying, bent over me in a hospital bed, handing me a warm seven-pound cherub swaddled in pink, round dark eyes below a tuft of brown hair, one set of locks pushing against the grain of the rest. We'll debate names. "Do you want to call her Peony?"

Phoenix will ask, invoking my favorite flower. But I'll look across the stark white recovery room at my mother-in-law. "I think her name should be Veronica, Viva for short."

"Meaning life," Phoenix will reply, nodding at the elegant suggestion.

Someday, a grown-up Viva will climb the attic stairs of the home where she's been raised and discover a box containing a sheaf of printed papers. Beneath the cover, she'd find a spiral-bound manuscript chronicling the challenges that could've shorn her parents apart. She'd settle onto a dusty crate and crack open the plastic cover. Her lips would move as she read the 12-point title on the face page, Goodbye, Orchid and its opening line: "Phoenix never believed today was goodbye."

The music slows. Phoenix takes me in his arms. He studies me. He lifts his hand to my chin, and as gentle as a kiss to a baby's forehead, he swipes his thumb below my jawline. I hadn't noticed until that moment. The back of my hand confirms it. My cheek is wet.

"I'm so happy," I say, contradicting the tears on my face.

"If this is happy, I'm scared to see sad," he says.

I giggle, and he joins me. "You always make me laugh," I say. The sun dips its head, nodding toasty rays over our wedding day.

"*Always* has a nice ring," he says. We sway to the crooning melody.

"And forever ..." But I don't have a chance to finish the sentence. My eyes close as his lips meet mine. They are so familiar. They are as tender as velvet. Before I completely lose myself in the kiss, one more thought floats across my consciousness. The thought warms me from the inside. To be able to give ourselves totally to the other, we each had to learn that we are not broken.

In fact, we are *all* whole.

No matter what.

Not a thing missing.

Before He Heard Her

"I won't let love disrupt, corrupt or interrupt me.
I want love to walk right up and bite me."

—Jack White, *Love Interruption*

RONAN

Before he heard her, he smelled her. Lemon. Honey. Wild lavender.

"Ronan? Is that you?"

The familiar timbre came from behind. He had time to tuck his folded cane beneath his raincoat. He hoped it wasn't visible.

Ronan gripped the subway handle and stared unseeing through his shades. Luckily, he'd donned his cool pair. The train swayed. Zoe's clothes brushed his as she rounded the space before him.

"Ronan. Oh my god. It's been what – six months?"

He knew exactly how long it'd been since he'd left his girlfriend. Half a year since the accident, so five months since they'd broken up. A different lifetime. The quiet nights and their missed anniversary should've inoculated him. Yet, even after all these fortnights, her voice rang as sweet as before.

"Aren't you going to say anything? Are you going to pretend you don't see me?"

A chuckle escaped. "I'm not pretending," he said, speaking the truth.

"Not funny. You can't ignore me when I'm standing right in front of you."

"Try me." He grinned despite the harrowing situation. It was one thing to keep a secret over the phone, another in person.

Her breath reached him, warming his neck where his shirt lay unbuttoned.

"I thought you'd moved to another country the way you disappeared. Are you still here in the city? Because that would make you an even bigger jerk than I thought you were," she said.

"I told you, you're better off without me."

The edge in her tone triggered memories like a high school song bringing back prom night. Snatches of their last call tumbled in. Zoe had started out full of disbelief. She'd been away on business for two months. "Have you met someone else?" she'd demanded. He couldn't tell her the truth and still protect her. "This makes no sense. We were in love, weren't we?" she'd asked. He'd wanted to erase her anguish then, as he did now.

He heard the air in her throat catch, bringing him back to the present.

"Hey … Ronan, are you okay?" Fabric swished as she raised her arm. Oh no, not the hand in front of the eyes thing. That was worse than anything. Uncalled for. Cliché. A test that he couldn't pass. Even if he couldn't witness himself being demeaned.

The train's automated conductor announced the next station.

"What the—" Zoe's tone ratcheted up towards drama. *The sound of her uncovering his secret.*

"This is my stop. Good '*seeing*' you," he said, his forefinger and middle finger forming an air quote to indicate he didn't mean 'seeing' literally. His own private joke. He broke away before she could discover his hampered capacity and lunged towards the door. Air released from the brakes and the doors slid open. He stumbled onto the platform, aiming for the exit. In the swirl of emotions, he hadn't even absorbed which station they'd entered. The echoes of footsteps against the tiled walls didn't sound familiar, like a station he'd previously traversed. Not since the accident, anyway. His commute tended to be unvaried. Here, among frenzied crowds, he didn't want to misstep onto the tracks. Or maybe he did.

"Ronan! Ronan!" she called, breathless, some yards behind him. Her heels tapped sharp and fast. Stilettos. Damn he wanted to see her. He could imagine the flash of red hair, the intensity of her hazel eyes.

He followed the sounds of the throngs, swept along with their motion. And his emotion. By some miracle, he fumbled his way through the turnstile. He'd worked hard to avoid this. This was never supposed to happen. And now he felt as lost as the day he'd woken in the hospital.

"Careful!" Zoe shouted, so close that she must just be an arm's length away.

But it was too late. His stride was fast and headlong. Until he struck something solid. The stairs felled him as easily as an axe splintering kindling. His knee twisted as he caught himself with the railing. His folded cane clattered onto the concrete, no longer hidden under his coat. The harsh echo reverberated in the cavernous station.

The crowd parted around him, commuters hurrying along their routes. Warm fingers grasped his elbow and helped him up.

"Are you hurt?" she asked, her worry sounding close to grief.

He tested some weight on his leg. "Nah. You know me. I'll do anything for attention."

She let go of his arm and chuckled. "You always made me laugh. Tell me you're not seeing anyone."

"I'm not really dating material."

"Shut it."

He heard a hard plastic edge scrape against the cement floor.

He put out his hand for his white cane, his face heating out of embarrassment for her seeing it. No question about it. His secret was eviscerated.

But instead of a lightweight cylinder, she shoved something small into his palm. He wrapped his fingers around the smooth circle topped by a sharp gemstone. "Oh."

Why today of all days, would she be wearing the promise ring he'd gifted her after the marathon? That summer morning, her mood had been buoyant, and her lips soft. It was the last time he'd raced.

"Here." She pressed the cool surface of his guide cane into his other hand.

"Thanks," he said. He tried to return the jewel and met air.

"Keep it," she said.

"It was for you."

"Not anymore." Her voice broke.

He pocketed the jewelry. It'd been the most dazzling piece in the store. One that shone almost as bright as Zoe's excitement when she was immersed in the beauty industry, attending fashion shows, or designing creative. She prized aesthetics, from the red lacquered bottoms of her Louboutins, to her twenty-one-step skin regimen. In the midst of all that perfection, there was no space for damaged goods.

"Do you have time for coffee?" she asked.

"Nope." There was no point. He clutched the handle and flung open the seeing eye cane's whole length. What did appearances matter now?

"How about something stronger?"

"It's eight in the morning," he laughed, and limped up the steps.

The tap of her heels kept pace with his. "I know an account up for grabs," she said. Smart. Talking shop would appeal to the entrepreneur in him.

"I'm not in design anymore," he said, trying to meter his bitterness. "How about you? You good? How was Korea?"

"K-beauty is amazing. Let me tell you about it over a bite to eat. You look too thin."

He shook his head. His cane found the top of the stairs. At street level, a chill mist wet his face.

"Oh c'mon. You owe me at least this. Weren't we serious? And you didn't even tell me the biggest thing to happen to you," she said.

"The biggest thing? Alright, you got me. The truth is, I pickpocketed your ring from a circus act."

She blew out some air. "Be serious for once. It's just five flippin' minutes."

He paused in the open air ten paces from the mouth of the station. His heart pounded, and his leg throbbed. This was ridiculous. A young able-bodied woman was not going to have problems keeping up with him.

He lifted his left arm to his face as if he was looking at a wristwatch. Even though he no longer had need for a watch. "Five. Starting now. And then we go our separate ways."

"Right here?! Can't we go somewhere? Sit for a bit?"

"Four minutes and forty seconds," he said.

"Um. Okay. Jesus."

He imagined Zoe staring at him and wondered what his expression revealed about the wreckage inside.

"I mean, I don't know if this is why you left me. But if it is... Is it? Is this why you broke up with me? Because I still had feelings. I still... Christ. Do you? Is this why?"

"Three minutes, fifty seconds," he responded.

"Stop being so stubborn." She smacked his arm. Then sounded guilty. "Oh god I'm sorry. What happened?"

"Bad accident. Three minutes."

He sucked a breath and inhaled citrus. She'd always been a cornucopia of scents – one for her hair, another along her neck, a third ...Stop.

She grew so quiet he wondered if she'd left. Then, she drew a finger along the stubble that lined his jaw. Instinct shuttered his eyes. She leaned against his chest, tiptoeing up, and brushed the hollow of one cheek with her lips. Lavender. Lemon.

"Two minutes, thirty seconds," she whispered, so close that he could feel her exhale.

He grasped for an antidote as rational thought slipped away. "Stiletto, your place is the other way," he said, trying to dissuade her with pragmatism.

"Ha. Stilettos, that's right. How'd you know?"

"Blind men can still hear."

The air grew silent.

"Is there any chance…that your vision will…?"

"Nope. This is it," he said.

"I'm sorry. But you know, it doesn't matter. Between us," she said.

He pulled back, the tightness in his throat making it hard to talk. "I was protecting you," he said.

"By breaking my heart?" her tone rose to incredulous.

"By not screwing up your perfect life."

"That's bull. You're no coward, but think about it, who are you really protecting?"

After months of friends and family treating him with kid gloves, afraid to upset him, Zoe's straight talk was like a slap upside his head. All those stories he'd told himself about why it was better to lie rewound themselves, now seen with a new lens.

He'd pictured her shirking away in horror, yet here she was, unwilling to leave him.

"Some days, this sucks," he said.

"And the days apart? Those suck worse," she said.

"Don't lie," he said but part of him wanted to hear this. Had needed hearing this since…

"Shh." She slipped her hands under his overcoat and melted into his warmth, encircling his waist until one cheek nestled against his chest.

He wrapped his free arm around her. His lips imprinted her lavender-scented hair.

There weren't even two minutes left to his self-imposed deadline.

"I've missed you so hard," he said, his voice unexpectedly gruff.

Ronan let his cane tumble to the sidewalk. Inside his pocket, he located Zoe's ring.

One minute?

There must be more.

ACKNOWLEDGEMENTS

While writing can seem like a solitary pursuit, the publication of a book is a team sport. *DearOrchid* results from the efforts of many people. First, heartfelt appreciation to the Purple Heart decorated heroes who helped shape and endorse my work: Sgt. Bryan Anderson, Navy Corpsman Doc Jacobs, and Sgt. Noah Galloway.

To pay homage to the experience of people with traumatic injuries and disabilities like these wounded veterans, sensitivity readers vetted the physical and emotional veracity of select stories. For this, deepest gratitude to Darryl Adams, Lex Gillette and author Laurie Alice Eakes.

Thank you to those who helped inspire me: my mother figures, childhood best friend, and my cats who accompany me for long hours at my keyboard.

Perspective is invaluable to any author. I appreciate the collaboration, unwavering belief, and keen editorial eye of Ellie Maas Davis, generous wisdom of publishing consultant Larry Kirshbaum, insightful beta reading feedback from Rachel Mack, Dorothy Lagg, Corrie Viola, Colleen Tucciarone, Debbie Andrian Tyler, and Bryan Anderson, proofreading by Alexander Van Den Hende, my aunt's memories of her sister, reminiscing about The Melody with reunion organizer Frank Gibson and Melody DJs, and the iconic Melody artwork of artist Lauren Curtis.

Thank you to each place that generously published or recognized the stories in this collection, including Claire Chao's *Remembering Shanghai* blog, Megan Morrison's *Nobody Reads Short Stories* podcast, and Writer's Digest Writing Competition.

You've heard the adage that a picture is worth a thousand words. The beautiful Getcovers design and Miblart formatting builds on the work of Kellie Emery and Sarah Flood-Baumann with guidance from creative director Steve Ginsberg. This book is designed to be a beautiful gift and keepsake, for a loved one or yourself. The final touch, the exterior page edge design, is by Painted Wings Publishing Services.

The reading and writing community is a welcoming place. Many authors and reviewers honored *Dear Orchid* by providing endorsements; their names appear in the upfront PRAISE section. I could fill pages with the names of book clubs, libraries, bookstores, bookstagrammers, agencies, podcasters, fellow authors, trade reviewers, industry groups, literary awards, media outlets, journalists, and influencers who have graciously supported, loved, endorsed and spread the word about my books. I am sending gratitude to each and every one of you who has hosted or attended one of my events, posted a review, gifted my books, and told others about my work. These are the greatest gifts you can give to an author. I'd likewise appreciate reviews for *Dear Orchid* (please post them on all major book outlets). Special thanks to my volunteers: Joan Nixon and Darla Ford for running my Facebook group and Tracy Francese for being willing to organize my email list.

No appreciation is complete without acknowledging loved ones who have supported each of my books. My humorous hubby, twins, family and friends have been unendingly supportive and understanding when I'm not available due to book commitments.

My husband, who has attended my book signings, helped take reader photos, and keeps our household running, says that he does whatever he can "to help me be the best person I can be." For this and so much more, I truly believe that Mr. Blue Sweater is a real-life hero right here at home.

Last but not least, thank you for the special connection between an author and her readers. Thank you for entrusting your time to me. Until next time, thank you, thank you.

DISCUSSION QUESTIONS

1. The book is crafted as love letters to "special people and moments in time." Which stories held the deepest resonance for you—and why?

2. The opening story, *Still, You're Tall,* provides an intimate view of one soldier's life as a wounded veteran. What does this story teach us about visibility, adaptation, and the quiet strength behind disability?

3. The heartbreaking conclusion of *My Wild Wild Twin* reveals the devastation of domestic violence. How do you rationalize the radically different outcomes of two lives that started in similar circumstances? Did the reunification with the author's friend's mother at the end of the story leave you with a hopeful feeling?

4. Stories like *Goldie Forever* and *Dear Luna Moth* explore our relationship with other living creatures. What do you think is our responsibility to the natural world? Did these stories remind you of losses in your own life?

5. Author Carol Van Den Hende shares vignettes from maternal figures who have shaped her life in her essay *Mother*. Which important people have influenced your pivotal moments? Who considers you a role model in their life?

6. A family secret is revealed in *Dear Secret Auntie* and *A Handful of Rice*. How does the trauma of families being torn apart echo in today's world?

7. In the *Meeting My Heroes* essays, we meet Purple Heart decorated veterans who inspired the *Goodbye Orchid* series, including Sgt. Bryan Anderson. What lessons do you take away from how Bryan faces his life-changing injuries? What can we learn from the way that Navy Corpsman Doc Jacobs and Sgt. Noah Galloway rebuilt their lives after their traumatic injuries?

8. In *Belonging in the Between*, the author shares the dichotomy between being considered Chinese in America, and Western in China. When or where have you ever felt that you didn't completely belong? Did the essay shift your assumption on how much fiction is autobiographical to an author's experience?

9. The story *Alone in Beijing* takes us to China, where the author lived during an international work assignment. How is the setting meaningful to Sam and David? What inner conflict do you think each character is dealing with?

10. If you have read the *Goodbye Orchid* trilogy, what did you want to know after the end of *Always Orchid*? Did *Let Us Begin at the End, Hungry Bird* provide satisfactory answers to those questions? And if you haven't yet read *Goodbye, Orchid,* what characters and relationships did the epilogue lead you to wonder about?

11. Award-winning short story *Before He Heard Her* has been performed aloud from Braille by blind Paralympian Lex Gillette. What emotions did the story evoke for you? How did you feel about the main character's dilemma, and his ex-girlfriend's response?

12. How do the essays and stories in *Dear Orchid* shed light on the author's sources of inspiration? How does this collection give you new insight into the *Goodbye Orchid* series? Where did you find the roots of the characters Orchid or Phoenix in these stories?

13. If you could write a letter to someone who changed your life (as the author does throughout), who would it be addressed to, and what might it say?

REFERENCES

My Wild, Wild Twin

Glaros, Tony. "Where We Live: Whiskey Bottom, brimming with history in Md.": *Washington Post,* April 18 2014.

https://www.washingtonpost.com/realestate/where-we-live-whiskey-bottom-brimming-with-history-in-md/2014/04/17/1ef8a402-b8e5-11e3-96ae-f2c36d2b1245_story.html

Dear Luna Moth

Shea, Susan. "The Short, Productive Life of the Luna Moth": *Adirondack Almanack*. July 10, 2019.

https://www.adirondackalmanack.com/2019/07/the-short-productive-life-of-the-luna-moth.html

A Handful of Rice, Dear Secret Auntie

Brown, Clayton D. "China's Great Leap Forward": *Association for Asian Studies* Volume 17:3 (Winter 2012): US, Asia, and the World: 1914–2012.

https://www.asianstudies.org/publications/eaa/archives/chinas-great-leap-forward/

Dear Handsome Hansen

"Chronicles of Thomas Covenant The Unbeliever": *Kirkus Reviews*. March 27, 2012.

https://www.kirkusreviews.com/book-reviews/stephen-r-donaldson/chronicles-of-thomas-covenant-the-unbeliever/

Dear Berliner

"Fall of Berlin Wall: How 1989 reshaped the modern world": *BBC*, November 4, 2019

https://www.bbc.com/news/world-europe-50013048

https://jwalkingin.com/2019/12/22/cold-war-train-to-berlin/

Dear Mr. Melody

Kelly, Bennett. "20 Years After Its Sudden Closure, New Brunswick Still Remembers The Melody Bar.": *New Brunswick Today*, March 20, 2021.

https://newbrunswicktoday.com/2021/03/20-years-after-its-sudden-closure-new-brunswick-still-remembers-the-melody-bar/

Essay No. 1: Doc Jacobs

Jacobs, Doc. *There and Back Again: Stories from a Combat Navy Corpsman* (2020) Koehler Books.

Torres, Ella. "Veteran who is an amputee gears up to climb Mount Kilimanjaro for charity:" ABC News, February 12, 2020.

https://abcnews.go.com/US/veteran-amputee-gears-climb-mount-kilimanjaro-charity/story?id=68916720

Essay No. 2: Noah Galloway

Galloway, Noah. *Living with No Excuses: The Remarkable Rebirth of an American Soldier* (2017) Center Street.

Galloway, Noah. "The Ultimate Men's Health Guy: 10th Anniversary Edition:" *Men's Health* Magazine, October 29, 2024.

https://www.menshealth.com/health/a62555016/ultimate-mens-health-guy-10th-anniversary/

Essay No. 3: Bryan Anderson

Anderson, Bryan. *No Turning Back: One Man's Inspiring True Story of Courage, Determination, and Hope* (2014) Berkley.

Carroll, Ward. "This triple amputee has taken Hollywood by storm:" We Are The Mighty. October 21, 2020.

https://www.wearethemighty.com/mighty-trending/this-triple-amputee-has-taken-hollywood-by-storm/

ABOUT THE AUTHOR

CAROL VAN DEN HENDE is an award-winning novelist who pens stories of resilience and hope. Her novels *Orchid Blooming, Goodbye, Orchid* and *Always Orchid* draw from her own Chinese American family's history, and have won 40+ literary awards, including the American Fiction Award, IAN Outstanding Fiction First Novel Award, and Royal Dragonfly Awards for Disability Awareness and Cultural Diversity.

Buzzfeed, *Parade*, and *Travel+Leisure* named "heartwarming, heartbreaking" *Goodbye, Orchid* a most anticipated read. *Glamour* Magazine recommended this "modern, important take on the power of love." *Woman's World* called *Always Orchid* "One of 7 Books You Won't Be Able to Put Down" and The International Pulpwood Queens selected the *Goodbye, Orchid* series as Books-of-the-Month three years in a row.

Carol's mission is unlocking optimism as a writer, speaker, global marketer, digital strategist, Board Trustee and Climate Reality Leader. One secret to her good fortune? Her humorous husband and twins, who prove that love really does conquer all.

www.ingramcontent.com/pod-product-compliance
Lightning Source LLC
Chambersburg PA
CBHW040226170726
48295CB00014B/819
* 9 7 8 1 9 5 8 2 2 3 0 7 9 *